Cognitive Behavioral Therapy

Beat Your Depression, Anxiety and Overthinking. Stop With Negative Attitude.

John Marllow

Table of Contents

Chapter 7: Changing Core Beliefs With CBT

Chapter 8: Work Through Procrastination With CBT

Conclusion

Introduction

Congratulations on purchasing *Cognitive Behavioral Therapy*, and thank you for doing so.

Alternative nature of therapies is getting accepted more and more than the mainstream nature of therapies in the medical community. One such alternative in the world of psychological treatment is CBT or cognitive behavioral therapy. It is a method of treatment that primarily concentrates on the solution, or you can say the required outcome. The treatment involves working backward in order to locate which specific ideas affect the patient's behavior. It involves the adjustment of such ideas to improve the overall behavior of the concerned patient. It has been proven completely safe and effective in several clinical trials. It can help someone to get better day by day, and also lead a better life. CBT will involve several sessions to get to more about the ideas and thought process of the patient.

The primary concept of this therapy is that although some of the actions can be controlled with the help of conscious thoughts, others are always the result of unconscious thoughts. All such experiences and thoughts generally stem from the surrounding where you have been brought up and where all your experiences have been shaped. In this guidebook, you will get to know about every aspect of CBT and how you can benefit from the same.

There are plenty of books on this subject on the market, thanks again for choosing this one! Every effort was made to ensure it is full of as much useful information as possible; please enjoy!

Chapter 1: What Is CBT?

Cognitive Behavioral Therapy or CBT is a kind of psychotherapeutic treatment that can easily help people learn to identify and alter disturbing or destructive thinking patterns. It helps in putting an end to all those thoughts that might have some kind of negative influence on emotions and behavior. The whole therapy concentrates on altering the negative nature of thoughts that might easily contribute to and also worsen depression, anxiety, and emotional difficulties. All such spontaneous negative thoughts can have some kind of detrimental influence on mood. With the help of CBT, all these thoughts are diagnosed, challenged, and then replaced with more realistic and objective thoughts.

History Of CBT

CBT was introduced during the 1960s. It was developed by a psychiatrist, Aaron Beck, who first noticed that some types of thinking could easily dedicate to emotional problems. Aaron Beck identified all such thoughts as 'automatic negative thoughts' and slowly developed the overall process of cognitive therapy. Where all other earlier behavioral therapies focused only on reinforcements, associations, and punishments in order to modify behavior, CBT addressed how feelings and thoughts can actually affect behaviors. Since that time, CBT is being identified as a very effective first-line option of treatment for several types of conditions and disorders.

CBT And Its Types

CBT comes along with a wide range of approaches and techniques that helps in addressing emotions, thoughts, and behaviors. All such can range from self-help materials to structured psychotherapies. There are various types of therapeutic approaches that are related to CBT.

- **Cognitive therapy:** To identify and modify distorted or inaccurate patterns of thinking, behaviors, and emotional responses.

- **DBT or dialectical behavior therapy:** It addresses behaviors and thoughts while involving various mindfulness and emotional regulation strategies.

- **Multimodal therapy:** It suggests that issues related to psychology need to be treated with the help of seven completely different but interconnected modalities – behavior, sensation, affect, cognition, imagery, biological/drug considerations, and interpersonal factors.

- **REBT or rational emotive behavior therapy:** It helps in identifying all kinds of irrational beliefs, throwing active challenges to all such beliefs, and ultimately learning to address and change all such patterns of thinking.

While every kind of cognitive behavior therapy takes some kind of different approach, all of them work in order to address all the underlying patterns of thinking that result in psychological distress.

Uses Of CBT

Cognitive behavior therapy can be used effectively as a short-term treatment to help people with certain specific problems and also to teach them to concentrate on present beliefs and thoughts. It is being used to treat several conditions like:

Depression

It is one of those disorders which are being treated successfully with the help of CBT. Anyone can get affected by depression. Generally, it gets triggered by a continuous series of stressful events. All such events will leave you with a feeling like there is no other option left where the whole world is standing against you. In this stage, people who suffer from depression might also opt for suicide as the only remedy. If you opt for regular therapy and your therapist suspects that you are actually thinking of suicide, they will take measures to make sure you are safe. It is essential to note that most people today live under huge rocks of stress at various points in their regular lives. It can be stated that all of this is a result of the present technological advancements. All of these stop people from escaping the daily routines. The only thing they know is work, where they leave their minds day and night.

The stress of this kind can result in negative thoughts. You might also start feeling extremely low. However, all of these cannot be called depression. You will have to be checked by a therapist or a psychologist to make sure you are depressed or not. CBT is put into use to treat cases of depression as it can effectively figure out why it is turning into an issue. The treatments will include various periods of consultation that will permit you and your therapist to discuss all the reasons behind your depressive behavior. All your issues and influences that you have experienced will be studied thoroughly for bringing the main issue right to the surface with the help of CBT. It can help in dealing with depression by isolating all the pre-disposed behavioral patterns and thoughts which result in a depressive cycle.

By effectively isolating and then altering your reactions and thoughts, the negative thoughts can be easily avoided, which tend to drive you crazy while being in a state of depression. The treatment is absolutely natural, and after completion, it will last for a lifetime.

Panic Disorder

There are people who might be pre-disposed to panic, even in the simplest situations. There might be no proper reason for the panic, or it might also be apparent quickly that it is linked to a certain stimulus. While panic is a kind of natural response to certain extreme incidents, panic disorder includes regular and repeated panic incidents. It can also result in some serious issues, for example, fear of going out of the house. Panic is nothing but a sudden surge of emotions that is linked to chemical responses to the presence of extreme danger. In fact, it is regarded as a natural part of your body getting ready to either flee or fight. It is a kind of survival instinct that has been a natural part of human nature for as long as we all have been living on this planet.

All those who suffer from panic disorders will also experience the same kind of stimulus as anyone else. But whenever they have an adrenaline rush and require to decide whether to flee or fight, they will tend to get overwhelmed by all their emotions. Some common signs of panic disorder involve nausea, sweating, trembling, and even heart palpitations. You might not need to get admitted to a hospital as you have an attack. They will not harm you physically, but the attacks can turn out to be very frightening at times. It has been found that in the

16

majority of cases, the panic stems from various behaviors in childhood where the mind has been conditioned to react in certain ways. It might be to freeze, despite the fact that the fear as any other kind of action might result in some fearful consequences. It is often the case when parents try to prevent their children from opting for certain actions without trying to explain why the same is not acceptable.

Your mind will associate itself with certain actions and scenarios with this kind of negative response. It will ultimately result in panic attacks whenever you find yourself in any kind of similar situation. Although you might be pre-disposed to panic if you come with certain types of genes, recent research depicts that upbringing might also play some significant role. CBT is put into use to reduce your fear gradually of a certain stimulus. It involves retracing all the influences which have resulted in extreme responses. It will help you to alter the way in which you think about all of them. All this will directly affect the response from your side that you have in similar situations. It is essential to get help with this very disorder as it might affect all your abilities in a serious way in the future.

Sleeping Difficulties

It has been found that there might be a link between sleeping difficulties and certain mental disorders. CBT has shown some positive effects on all those people who suffer from poor and irregular patterns of sleeping. Lack of sleep might lead to various other serious effects on your daily life, along with continuous tiredness all throughout the day. It might also prevent you from completing all your tasks effectively. Insomnia or irregular sleeping patterns might be the result of various factors:

- Stress is regarded as one of the primary causes as your mind never gets the chance to relax. Remaining 'wired' constantly can make sleep very difficult.

- Your area of sleep is not being designed properly. It might include too little or too much light, an uncomfortable bed, or continuous noise from the surrounding.

- Medication or certain types of physical illness that affects the ability to sleep properly.

- Issues related to mental health that might make you feel tired, extremely tired to sleep, or even scared to fall asleep.

- CBT can readily help in dealing with all these issues to bring back your good night's sleep.

CBT is also being used for treating other issues such as:

- Anger issues
- Addictions

- Anxiety

- Personality disorders

- Bipolar disorder

- Phobias

- Eating disorders

CBT is highly focused and goal-oriented. Your therapist will play an extremely active role. You will also have to cooperate with your therapist to achieve all your goals quickly. Using CBT for dealing with all such issues will be discussed in detail in the upcoming chapters.

Impact

The concept behind CBT is that feelings and thoughts play an important role n shaping your behavior. For instance, a person who keeps thinking about plane crashes, accidents on the runway, or any other kind of air disaster might try to stay away from air travel as a result. The primary goal of CBT is to teach others that although they cannot control every aspect present around them, they can still take complete control of the way they interpret and also deal with several things around them. CBT has turned out to be very popular in the last few years among both treatment professionals and mental health consumers. Some of the definite reasons behind this include:

- By being aware of the unrealistic and negative thoughts that dampen our moods and feelings, we can start being engaged in healthier patterns of thinking.

- It might act as a great and effective treatment option for the short-term.

- CBT can help people deal with various types of emotional distress that do not need any kind of psychotropic medication.

- It is much affordable than other types of mental health therapy.

- It is supported empirically and has helped patients to overcome various maladaptive behaviors.

In short, cognitive behavioral therapy is a simple and easy therapy option that can provide instant results within a short span of time.

Strategies Of CBT

People often experience sudden feelings or thoughts that compound or reinforce faulty beliefs. All such beliefs can lead to problematic behaviors that tend to affect various life areas, including romantic relationships, family, academics, and work.

Identifying The Negative Thoughts

It is essential to learn how feelings, thoughts, and situations can lead to maladaptive behaviors. The overall process can be very tough, specifically for all those who struggle with introspection. However, ultimately it can lead to insights and self-discovery that are important parts of the whole treatment process.

Practicing New Skills

It is required to start with the practice of new skills that can then be used for real-world situations. For instance, an individual with a substance use disorder can start practicing new coping skills and rehearsing various ways to deal with or avoid social situations that might trigger a serious relapse.

Setting Goals

Goal setting is an essential step in the process of recovery from mental illness. It can provide you with effective help to make certain changes in order to improve your life and health. At the time of CBT, a therapist can provide you with the required help with skills of goal-setting by teaching how to effectively identify the goals, differentiate between long-term and short-term goals, set up specific, attainable, measurable, time-based, and relevant goals, and to concentrate on the whole process as much as the final outcome.

Problem Solving

Learning essential skills to solve problems can help to solve and identify all those problems that tend to arise from stressors in life, both small and big. It can also help to reduce the impacts of the negative nature of the physical and psychological illness. Solving problems in CBT generally involves five steps:

- Identification of the problem

- Generation of a list of possible solutions

- Evaluation of weaknesses of each of the solution

- Evaluation of strengths of each of the solution

- Implementation of a definite solution

Self Monitoring

Often called diary work, self-monitoring is a very important part of cognitive behavioral therapy that includes tracking of symptoms, behaviors, or even experiences at times. You will have to share all of these with your therapist. It can help to provide your therapist with all the required information to provide you with the best treatment. For instance, in eating disorders, self-monitoring might involve keeping proper track of the habits of eating along with the feelings or thoughts that went along during the consumption of that snack or meal.

Gradual Progression

In most cases, CBT is a kind of gradual process that helps an individual take certain incremental steps in the direction of behavior change. For instance, a person who suffers from social anxiety can start by imagining various anxiety-provoking situations in social gatherings. The next probable step might involve practicing conversations with family, friends, and acquaintances. As you progressively work in the direction of a larger goal, the overall process will seem much less daunting. The goals will also be much easier to be achieved.

Benefits Of CBT

There are several benefits of CBT that can be identified gradually.

- It can be as effective as any other medication that is used to treat some serious mental health issues. It has been found that approximately 7% of adults in the US suffer from a serious depressive disorder every year. The common symptoms include loss of interest in all those things that were enjoyed previously, lower levels of energy, isolation, and development of physical diseases. When

CBT is followed, the patterns of negative thinking can be reconstructed. It will help in relieving moderate cases under the supervision of a therapist in the same way as medication does.

- The therapy does not involve much time to be completed when compared with other forms of therapy. All those patients who undergo CBT will have to opt for an individual session, which will last for half an hour to one-hour maximum. It depends on the problems involved. You will have to meet your therapist approximately once every week or once every alternate week. The majority of CBT cases last for about 20 weeks or even less than that. Even there are patients who can get done with their therapy within just five weeks. Unlike other talkative therapies, CBT will allow you to experience the results within a short time.

- There are various types of tools and sessions available in CBT, depending on the issues. Multiple tools are available for every patient to put into use as they work towards restructuring their patterns of thinking. Even there are group sessions available that will make you understand that you are not alone. Also, road trips are included in the therapy at times. It is primarily because the aim is to provide you with the needed help to work in various ways that seem comfortable and natural to you.

- As you opt for cognitive behavioral therapy, the therapist will not be telling you what you need to do. They will work in cooperation with you to properly figure out a solution for all your difficulties. That indicates you will have to identify the issues on a personal level and then invest everything in yourself to bring about the necessary changes in life. It will help you to find out different solutions for different problems. It is nothing but a collaborative effort. As the process involves collaborative effort, you can find more accountability in the whole process. When you jump into something hand in hand with a supportive partner, your chances of succeeding doubles.

- It is useful for any age group. Both adults and children can benefit from CBT when used in the correct way. The expectations will be the same for any age group. As long as there are a willingness and capacity to make some changes in life, CBT will provide you with various solutions that can be used for the treatment of existing problems. In fact, taking out some time to talk about an issue or a situation is enough to show experience some effective results. It is because there are people who tend to keep tough situations internalized. It results in suffering as they do not try to share all their concerns with someone else. CBT is an effective way to establish trust in oneself and others while also working to break through the negative cycles, along with the destructive influences of life.

CBT And Its Potential Pitfalls

Regardless of the wide range of benefits, there are certain pitfalls that make people think twice about CBT.

- The overall change might turn out to be difficult. Initially, there are patients who will suggest that as they recognize that some of their thoughts are not healthy or rational, only by becoming aware of all those thoughts will not make it easy for them to alter.

- The complete therapy that involves CBT is very structured. CBT does not tend to concentrate on the underlying unconscious resistances to alter as much as some other approaches like psychoanalytic psychotherapy. It is generally best-suited for all those who tend to be more comfortable with a focused and structured approach. The therapist will also take some important instructional role.

- All those who are suffering from irrational and unhealthy thinking patterns need to be willing to change. For the best effects of CBT, and for the therapy to be a success, the patients need to be willing and ready to spend some time along with some effort to analyze their feelings and thoughts. Such a form of homework and self-analysis might turn out to be difficult. However, it is a superb way to learn in detail how internal states can impact outward behavior.

Chapter 2: Identify The Problem

Identifying the problem is an essential step in cognitive behavioral therapy. The best way to describe the functioning of CBT is to learn in detail how a therapist might go through with a patient. The process of identifying the problem along with solving the same is done in various stages. Let's have a look at them.

Stage 1: Assessment

During the very first sessions of CBT, a therapist will try to find out what nature of problems is trying to trouble the concerned patient. The therapist will also try to explore all the goals of the patient – what would he/she want to be after the therapy ends? The therapist of CBT will opt for an assessment to discuss all or some of the following:

- Asking direct and open questions to help the patient open up about their problems. For example, "You can tell me why you are here," "What are those things that have been giving you problems recently?"

- Creating a list of problems with the help of the patient. It would also involve thinking about the essentiality of each of the problems. For example, "Now that both of us have made a proper list of all those things that have been troubling you, can we arrange them in order to make sure how much each of them interferes with the course of your life?"

- The therapist would like to generate measurable and specific goals with the patient. All of this is done by concentrating on all those behaviors that the patient desires to change. For example, "What exactly would you have been doing differently if the problems were not problems anymore?"

- Another great way that a therapist might use to identify the problems is to opt for structured interviews and questionnaires. It can help to assess the absence or presence of difficulties or symptoms.

- The therapist might opt for asking various questions along with a discussion about past and current suicidal actions and thoughts. For example, "Do you have thoughts of ending your life or hurting yourself?"

-

Assessment Technique #1: Concentrating On Certain Events

A great way to get to know the problems of the client is to pay sheer attention to certain events that took place recently. In short, the therapist would try to identify proper details like, "Last day when I came across anyone who seemed like my attacker I was frozen at the spot with fear" rather than, "I just feel so low all the time that I am unsure whether it is of any worth." It might involve some work in order to extract specific details from certain examples like the latter one. The primary reason why cognitive behavioral therapy concentrates on certain events is that our lives are designed for certain moments that are al chained together. We all tend to live our lives moment by moment. We also try to feel all our feelings in that exact same way.

We all have the habit of telling stories to ourselves like, "I had the worst and the most boring day of my life." However, the chances are that your whole day included some boring moments, along with some exciting ones as well. If we just try to concentrate on our behaviors and thoughts, all of these will tend to take place moment by moment. We will end up missing all the important parts in case we just try to glossing over the details. Problems from your past might not tend to be an issue any longer is the main cause why the therapy procedure concentrates on all those aspects that are small problems now. Also, when devastating things took place in our past, the difficulty/suffering – which we all try to get relieved from, happens in the current moment. A major primary assumption made by CBT is that everything that takes place in the moment contributes to our sufferings. The last positive side of stressing on present situation is that we often have better of it, which indicates we can have the opportunity to explore the same in detail.

Assessment Technique #2: Breaking Down Every Moment Into Important Components

After you have successfully discovered a particular and latest event, now it is time to divide the same into several components that are manageable. It might involve:

- **Situation:** What happened? Who were there? When all of it happened? What was the location?

- **Cognitions:** What exactly went through your mind at that moment?

- **Trigger:** What exactly was going on prior to the occurrence of the issue?

- **Emotions:** What were your feelings?

- **Sensations in the body:** What sensations or feelings you noticed in your body?

- **Responses or actions:** What was your response? What was done on your part to cope with the problem?

The primary reason why therapists of CBT opt for assessments by breaking down events into various components is that the approach of this therapy believes that all such components are linked to one another. One of the components will affect others in various ways. Trying to make proper sense of all the connections is termed as case conceptualization.

Stage 2: Case Formulation

It is a different thing to address a problem. However, to figure out the proper solutions, we will have to:

- Understand in detail what is helping the problem to stay alive

- Find a bunch of proper ways to put an end to the same

The therapists of CBT put into use a technique known as case formulation or case conceptualization. It helps in understanding how a problem tends to operate. A formulation is nothing but a simple model or a bunch of hypotheses. A therapist will develop his/her own set of hypotheses, will properly explore any of the hypotheses if the patient has. He/she will then try to figure out proper paths along with the patient to test the correctness of the hypotheses.

CBT Tries To Focus On Consequences And Relationships

While taking into account any kind of problem, a CBT therapist will aim to collect information related to: when/where the problem takes place, the triggers behind the same, sensations in the body, emotions, along with behaviors that result in the problem. The next big step is to find out the relationships between all the components. As a rule in general:

- Everything that you notice might easily trigger all your thoughts. Some of the triggers for developing thoughts involve incidents, body sensations, everything around you, memories, and other thoughts. You might also think about anything. So, it can be said that anything might turn out to be a possibly triggering all your thoughts.

- Your thoughts slowly result in feelings. An important CBT insight is that how we opt for interpreting various situations can affect the way we feel for them. All such interpretations can happen automatically and quickly. They can also get affected by several other events or things that took place in the past.

- All your actions lead to certain consequences. It is somewhat similar to the third law of Newton – "Every action comes with an equal and opposite reaction." All your actions are same – all that you do in your life also comes with consequences. A portion of the consequences might be of intentional nature, while others might be not. Opting for questions like, "What were the exact consequences of acting out in that way?" is a very common CBT step. Analyzing the consequences provides therapists with the needed help to properly find out why the patterns of problems tend to persist longer than expected otherwise.

CBT Focuses On What Makes Certain Problems Persist

A complete fire requires three components to get started: fuel, oxygen, and heat. The time for which all these components are present, the burning of fire will continue. With this idea, the firefighters can decide which component to aim for. Relying on the nature of the fire, the firefighters might decide to:

- Cutoff oxygen supply by spraying CO_2

- Remove the available fuel

- Spray water to cut off the heat

The process of CBT also tend to examine problems in the same method: the main concentration is on the maintaining components. Similar to fire, it is not that essential to find out the factor that started it. However, you will have to figure out all those things that keeps it burning. Therapists of CBT are trained to give all their focus to any kind of sequence that seems like to be in a continuous loop. There are several ways in which problems of humans can actually be taken care of. Some of the most common factors that might maintain the problems in place are:

- **Avoidance:** It might be both internal and external. One of the difficulties caused by avoidance is that it does not provide us the chance to figure out how well we could actually have coped with the problem if not avoided. For example, "Sam was so anxious all the time about something catastrophic taking place that he did not even leave his house. He also avoided getting close to the exit door."

- **Biased memory:** It indicates recalling only a portion of any story. All those who suffer from anxiety will always find it very easy to keep in mind threatening information automatically. All those who suffer from depression might tend to have 'over general' memory. They also face difficulty in recalling certain events.

- **Reinforcement:** We tend to repeat all those actions that leave us back with a good feeling. It might happen that the behavior is not healthy for us in the long run.

- **Safety behaviors:** It includes all those things that all of us try to stay away from that we think might be a catastrophe. Similar to avoidance, a basic primary problem that is related to safety behaviors is - they might stop us from figuring out that the negative outcome might not have happened ever.

- **Biased attention:** All your attention will seem to be biased when you notice only a portion of any incident or event. One of the basic problems is that all of us try to be attentive only to our failures. We try to move our eyes away from the successes. All of us just tend to be biased with a fixed image of ourselves.

- **Repetitive thinking:** It indicates sticking to all the persisting problems, along with asking questions such as, "Why is my life always like this?" A range of thought processes will not result in the types of answers that can actually help all of us. It has been discovered that 'How' questions are more helpful than 'Why' questions.

- **Self-criticism:** It indicates telling yourself for all those things that you are or have done. In some of the cases, a small portion of self-criticism can turn out to be motivating. However, in the majority of cases, it is being done in a tone of punishment instead of being encouraging.

How Pieces Fit Together

It has been found that maintaining components might come together in some l ways to develop issues/problems. We will have a detailed look at a range of common problems in this section and will also learn in detail about the factors that help them persist.

Anxiety

All those who suffer from panic attacks tend to experience sensations of ambiguous nature in the body at times. They feel that the presence of such sensations might indicate that something terrific is going to happen. Thinking of this type leads to strong reactions of emotions along with certain attempts to cope of understandable nature. The biased thinking, avoidance, and selective attention act as essential maintaining components for panic.

Depression

Similarly, it has been found that all those who experience low mood tends to have changes in behavior, along with their thinking. All such changes help depression to be in its place.

Mixed problems

There are people who tend to struggle with more than one single problem at a time. CBT is flexible in nature. Putting into use the same building blocks, it can provide a framework to help understand the problems so that we can develop our own framework.

Stage 3: Symptom Monitoring

Once the therapist and patient have decided
which problems or problem to focus on, along
with some idea regarding what might be keeping
the issues in place, the process of CBT
emphasizes on proper monitoring of the
symptoms, along with the problems. Right in the
similar way as thoughts might turn out to be
biased, the impressions regarding whether CBT
can be useful might fall under bias as well.
Therapists of CBT might make certain
assumptions regarding the way the therapy is
functioning. It can also be mistaken easily. The
bias of this nature can be easily won over by
measuring the problems, along with the
symptoms regularly. It also involves checking
with the patient regularly what they actually
think about the effectiveness of the therapy.

Symptom monitoring is very easy as keeping a
count of how often a problem or something
occurs. For example, keeping a count of how
often an individual with experience panic attacks
or keeping a count of how often a person
suffering from OCD tends to perform any of their
related compulsions.

Stage 4: Techniques For Change

After you have assessed the problems, explored
all the possible goals, and have taken some

guesses regarding why the problems persist, the time has come to opt for some action. At times, the stage of conceptualizing the case alone can act single-handedly to bring in the required motivation to change. Individuals might often feel relieved by speaking regarding an issue or problem, might feel helpful by understanding the way it tends to operate, and often opt for changes in their lives.

Techniques To Change The Way You Feel By Altering All Those Things That You Think

Another essential intervention in CBT is to provide support to the patients to understand, followed by changing the not so helpful patterns along with thinking type. A basic way in which therapists help patients to alter the way they tend to think is by putting into use worksheets of CBT. It helps in scaffolding their monitoring of thoughts, along with practice of thought modification. The first step to change what we think is to properly figure out what goes on inside our minds. It is known as monitoring of thoughts. The next big step is to effectively study the helpfulness, along with accuracy of all those thoughts once patients can properly figure out the thoughts of negative nature. It is known as cognitive restructuring.

Identifying Automatic Thoughts

Some feelings might seem predictable in some situations, whereas others might seem puzzling. At times, we feel some emotions out of the blue, too strong for all those things that are going on. The primary key to understand feelings is to identify all the thoughts associated with them. Thoughts tend to influence most of our world experiences, along with our emotional experiences. Automatic thoughts are those thoughts that arise in our minds automatically during the course of the day. Often, we are unaware that we are actually having thoughts. However, with a bit of practice and instruction, we can learn to identify all of them. As a result, we will learn to handle our behavior and mood in a better way.

Why Focus On Thoughts?

Our minds are machines that keep processing thoughts. It also creates and sifts through thousands of ideas in a day. If we had to attend to all of them, we would have been flooded with information. Most of the thoughts enter our brain and also leaves without us being aware of the same. Our minds are quite good at filtering out all those thoughts that are not that important and try to focus on all those that seem to be more salient. The process functions well the majority of the time. However, at times we tend to focus on less important information while filtering out the important ones. For example, job performance review. We try to filter out all the praise and just concentrate on those areas where we need to improve. It is known as negative filtering. It indicates filtering out everything other than the negative information.

The example in this section can highlight a very powerful and common dynamic: Automatic thoughts come with the potential to trigger negative emotions of a negative nature. Generally, we tend to be more aware of all the emotions rather than the thoughts that actually trigger them. But in most cases, our automatic thoughts play the most important role in determining how we feel, not the situation itself. As you learn to examine all these thoughts, it will allow you to better deal with and understand your emotions. You will get the chance to modulate them before they turn into something very overwhelming or intense.

How To Identify?

There are people who find this skill quite tough at first but get a catch on it quickly. The primary key to identify automatic thoughts is to determine what comes into your mind when any emotion arises. For instance, Sam discovered on social media that one of his friends, John, has arranged a party with some of his friends and has not invited him. Sam will immediately feel a huge pit in his stomach and identify that emotion as sadness. At that exact moment, he asked himself, "What exactly is going through my mind?" He was able to properly identify all these thoughts:

- John does not like me anymore.

- No one invites me to anything.

- No one in my friend circle likes me.

Given the extreme extent of all these thoughts, a feeling of sadness can be understood. By writing out his thoughts, Sam was able to process all of them differently and find out how extreme all of them were. The exercise also helped him to see that he was actually making some broad assumptions that he did not believe wholeheartedly. Afterward, Sam felt better, and some of his profound sadness also lifted. The entire process of recognizing all thoughts and thoughts is what is known as metacognition. It is the process that helps in developing awareness, along with an understanding of all our thoughts. As in the mentioned example, becoming aware merely of thought processes can help us create a distance from all the reflexive cognitive responses and reevaluate them.

It is quite hard to overstate how powerful exactly this tool can be to change our behavior and feelings. Another great way to uncover hidden thoughts is by asking yourself, "What can be the possible part of this, and why?" In this case, the possible answer might be that Sam believes he never gets called to anything, and that is quite tough as he concludes that no one likes him. Lastly, if all of these methods do not work for you on getting some results, you can try to identify the exact emotion and then just work backward.

Identifying Intrusive Thoughts

Having negative and obsessive ideas might turn out to be a great source of suffering. It is among those things that can easily intensify the vicious cycle of anxiety. It might dig you deeper into your hole as you try to surround yourself with impulses, images, along with unhelpful reasoning that can cloud your sense of control completely. In all such cases, hearing, "Just calm down. There is nothing to worry about all those things that have not happened yet," cannot help. Whether you actually like the fact or not, but your mind is an unlimited idea factory. Unfortunately, everything that it produces cannot always help you to achieve all your goals or even feel better. We all have some unhelpful and pretty absurd ideas every day. But under absolutely normal conditions, we do not provide this reasoning with too much power. In place of that, we try to prioritize helpful and encouraging thoughts.

Now, as we go through intense periods of anxiety or stress, intrusive thoughts will try to be frequent. Usually, we also give all these thoughts excessive power than they actually deserve.

Techniques To Deal With Intrusive Thoughts

There are several possible ways in which we can deal with intrusive thoughts.

Thought Records

Thought records permit us to apply some logic to all our mental processes. Try to think of someone who is always afraid to lose his job. Overnight, he will get obsessed with the very fact that his management thinks he is not doing well. The cycle might end up causing some self-fulfilling prophecy. That is, by trying to think about everything where he could go wrong, very soon, he will just end up doing the same. In order to get a better sense of control, coherence, and balance, nothing can be more helpful than creating records of all our invasive thoughts. All that it takes is to write down all your negative ideas that keep appearing in your mind. Then you will have to work on its truth.

Scheduling Positive Acts

Try to schedule rewarding activities during the course of the day. Something as very simple as "some quality time for yourself" can provide you with various positive results. It can prevent you from overthinking. All such activities can be very brief and simple, for example, going out for a coffee with a close friend. Try to give some break to yourself. You can start reading books, listen to good music, and many more.

Hierarchy Of Your Concerns

Intrusive thoughts are somewhat like smoke from a long chimney. It is nothing but the heat of something that is constantly burning deep inside us. That very internal fire is built of all our unresolved problems that tend to worsen with passing time. The very first step to control the concentration of all your feelings, thoughts, and anguish is to clarify them properly. How can you clarify them? It can be done by building a hierarchy of problems. It is nothing but a scale of concerns that are arranged from low to high. You can start by writing down all those things that tend to concern you. You will have to visualize all the chaos that is present inside you, just like a brainstorm. Next, try to establish a hierarchy, starting with those that you think of as small problems. End the hierarchy with all those that leave you paralyzed with stress and anxiety. After you have established a visual order, try to reflect deeply on each of the points. You will have to start thinking rationally and also come up with some solution for each.

Emotional Reasoning

It is a very common kind of distortion. For instance, if you have a bad day and end up being frustrated, you will start visualizing your life as a dark and endless tunnel. So, another important technique that you must learn to be used daily is objectivity. You cannot forget the fact that all your emotions are not indicative of any objective truth all the time. They are mere momentary moods that you have to understand and manage.

Stopping Intrusive Thoughts

Whether you want it or not, there will always be certain situations that will tempt you to fall into the hole of intrusive thoughts once more. One of the most effective ways to be attentive to all these situations is to maintain a diary. Doing something as simple and easy as writing down all your thoughts and feelings every day will permit you to be more conscious of everything around you. Just write down everything that comes to your mind. Try to describe all those situations when you felt some specific feelings. Perhaps there will be habits, scenarios, or people who can make you feel vulnerable or just lose control. As you keep records of your day, you will get the chance to see everything as they actually are. You will get the power to stop yourself from having some negative reaction to all of them.

Chapter 3: Learn Goal Setting

"I require to get in shape," "I want to make my life more balanced and just be happy." Statements of this type are quite familiar to every one of us. The majority of us are quite good at properly identifying the changes that we want to see in our lives. But effecting all of these changes is quite difficult than actually identifying what they are. It is something like, "Easier said than getting it done." Sometimes we just get overwhelmed by the huge size of the goals that we set in front of us, and we cannot just figure out where to start from. At times, we try our best to achieve some of our goals; however, it does not seem to work out. In all such situations, it is very easy to start feeling discouraged and just give up.

When Are Setting Goals Helpful?

Goal setting can be helpful in various sectors of life. For example, searching for a new job, starting with a new hobby, saving money for foreign trips, and many more. However, setting goals can also be very helpful as you try to address behavioral or emotional difficulties. It is considered a great tool that is often being used in CBT or cognitive behavioral therapy. For instance, a person who is depressed in life and has isolated himself/herself can work with his/her therapist towards a steady goal to increase the strength and number of friendships.

A person experiencing excessive anxiety because of his/her job can work with a CBT therapist to explore other career sectors or just make some more time for leisure or relaxation. As the strategies of goal setting are often used in cognitive behavioral therapy, this kind of therapeutic approach can be very helpful for all those who actually struggle to meet their set goals, no matter what they might be.

Four-Step Method

The goal-setting approach in this section is completely based on the methods that are used in CBT. However, they can be useful for anyone.

- **Identifying goals:** It might sound very simple, but identifying a proper and clear goal is very important. In order to get started, try to ask yourself, "What is my actual goal?"

- **Identifying the starting point:** After you have identified the goal successfully, try to take stock of the current state of things with respect to your goal. Try to be honest and just ask yourself, "Where does everything stand now?"

- **Identifying the steps:** It can be quite easy to forget that attaining a goal is accomplished rarely in just one single step. Try to break down your set goal into several chunks simply by identifying all the steps that it would actually take to get from the starting point to the finish line of the goal. Start asking yourself, "How can this be broken down to make it seem more achievable?" Try to keep each of the steps as small as possible. Always keep in mind that small steps are always more achievable than the bigger ones. As you feel successful after accomplishing smaller steps along your way, it can help in keeping you motivated in the direction of your goal. Also, when if you succeed in surpassing the goal for a small step, you can still feel proud of going ahead. All you just require to do is to put all the steps in proper order.

Ask yourself, "What could possibly be the first step in the direction of my goal?" followed by "What should be the next step?" and just go ahead. Try to focus more on the early steps, and do not forget to pay attention to the possible obstacles. Give your best to think about what could possibly come in the way of accomplishing all the steps that you have laid out. No one in this world can properly predict all the potential barriers or obstacles. However, as you consider all these now, you can be better at working around problems as they tend to arise.

- **Getting started:** The final step is to get started with the first step that you have set in your plan of action.

Setting Up Goals

Now that you have some proper understanding of the point where to start from, it is now time to set up some goals to effectively understand where exactly you are willing to end up. You will have to develop goals that are achievable and specific as well. Whenever researchers try to design some experiments, they have to determine beforehand how they will come to know that whether they have successfully met all the objectives. For example, "Patients who consume drug A will start getting better," but "All those who consume B dose of drug A will effectively show some definite reduction in the symptoms of illness C than all those patients who took a placebo, as measured by X, Y, and Z." What does it exactly mean to get better? How are you going to know that if you can actually improve?

If you could just skip ahead to the time when you have practiced all the skills along with techniques in this book for a great deal of time, and every possible thing went exactly the way you hoped for, how is your life going to be different? What will have been changed exactly? Are there any particular things that you would be able to do that seemed too tough before? Are

there some particular things that you would want
to be able to do?

Step #1: Start writing down your primary goals.
These will be the changes in every general issue
that you have described above. For instance, if
one of the issues is "sadness or low mood," your
ultimate goal might be to improve your mood.

Step #2: As you are already done with your
general issues, you will now have to make your
primary goal more specific in nature. What does
the goal mean to you? How are you going to
know if you have successfully met the goal? Try
to use your particular descriptions of the issues
to guide you properly. For instance, if one of the
particular descriptions of any issue just like
anxiety is that 'you keep avoiding situations that
tend to make you nervous, such as in places
where you do not know anyone,' one of your
proper goals might be to 'accept more invitations
and start attending parties, even when you do
not know anyone out there.' Another great
proper goal might be to 'arrange a party at your
place and ask your friends to invite each of their
friends who are not known to you.'

Step #3: Start highlighting all those actions that
tend to be consistent with all your goals so that
you can get a definite idea of whether you are
getting closer to them or not.

Below are some of the examples that will help
you to complete your own sheet of goal-setting.

Goal #1: <u>Improved assertiveness</u>

Specific goals: I would like to express all my opinions more, along with telling my friends what I actually think. I want to start speaking up at work meetings. I want to ask someone for an outing or a date, or even start some social plans with my close friends. I want to text or call a friend of mine just out of the blue to have some chat. I would like to believe that I do have something always to dedicate to conversations.

Actions consistent with the goals: Speaking up in professional and social settings, starting social plans and social contacts.

Goal #2: <u>Increases self-esteem</u>

Specific goals: I want to start feeling better regarding myself, along with thinking that I am worthy of everything. I would like to know that every work I do has some value. I want to understand and focus on all my strengths instead of focusing only on the weaknesses that are visible to me. I want to start engaging more with all my friends in place of just trying to stay away from socializing as I might start feeling bad.

Actions consistent with the goals: Trying to connect with all friends and trying to socialize, creating lists of all my strengths and just reminding myself about them, along with trying even harder in all my work.

SMART Goals

The acronym SMART is an essential part of trying to identify proper steps and goals. It stands for:

Specific: You will have to try to be as specific as you can so that you can successfully tell when you have properly completed a step or a goal. "Get more workout" is a bit vague, but "Go for a short walk around the house three days every week" can be ticked off easily in your large list of steps.

Measurable: Making your steps and goals measurable indicates that you can keep track of your progress with time. As mentioned in the above example, specifying "three days every week" can provide you with a proper way to measure the overall changes in your habits of exercising.

Achievable: You will have to ensure that the goals you have opted for can be attained in real life. It might be great to feel inspired of winning millions of dollars in a lottery. However, it is very unlikely that you will actually achieve that specific goal. It does not even matter how well you devise your plans as long as your goals are not achievable.

Relevant: Ensure that your chosen goal is properly in line with the issues you are actually trying to treat or address. Learning how to be a great public speaker is a superb goal. However, it might not be the most relevant one if your main goal is to make more new friends.

Timely: You will have to make sure that 'now' is a great time to start working on the goals. For instance, having the goal to clean the attic might be helpful, but perhaps it might be not if you are still dealing with back problems or surgery.

Troubleshooting If Goals Are Not Met

While pursuing your goals, if you figure out that you are unable to complete a specific step along the road, try to have a closer look at the same. It might be possible that the step was huge. So, do not feel scared to break the same down further and just start again from there. It might also be that the particular step was not much SMART from the very start. Try to see if it can be reworked so that you can tackle the same again.

Chapter 4: How Does CBT Help With Low Self-Esteem?

Our self-esteem can be regarded as the opinion that we all have of ourselves. All those who tend to suffer from low self-esteem are found to be often plagued with various feelings of awkwardness, frustration, and worthlessness. All such feelings can leave these people more susceptible to various issues related to mental health, such as social anxiety and depression. However, how are you going to know whether you are suffering from problems of low self-esteem? In this chapter, we will focus on low self-esteem and how CBT can help in various situations.

What Is Low Self-Esteem?

Your self-opinion is nothing but the opinion that you hold for yourself. When you have a good level of self-esteem, you will tend to start thinking in a positive way about yourself. You will start thinking optimistically regarding your life in general. As you encounter several challenges in life, your confidence level boosts up that you can easily get done with the task or challenge. People who possess healthy self-esteem will know that they are valuable. They will also be capable of naming at least one or some of their positive characteristics. For example, "I am a kind person," "I am a very good friend," "I am a great father," or "I am very honest." As you have low self-esteem, you will start seeing the world, yourself, and also your future in a critical and negative way. As you start encountering challenges in life, you will tend to doubt whether you can actually complete the task or meet the challenges.

You will tend to avoid challenges or tasks as much as you can when your self-esteem is low. You might also start talking harshly in your own mind. For example, you might tell yourself, "You are very stupid," "You will never be capable of managing such tasks," or "I do not really amount to anything in life." You might start feeling sad, anxious, unmotivated, or low. No one in this world is born with unhealthy or low self-esteem. It tends to develop with time as a result of the various types of experiences that we have during our lifetime. Right at the center of low self-esteem are all those opinions and beliefs that we tend to hold about ourselves. We just tell ourselves various stories regarding who we actually are and tend to form untrue conclusions regarding ourselves. All such opinions can actually be fixed, although they the 'truths' for all our lives. In actuality, though, they are mere labels or stories. They do not even capture the overall truth of who we truly are.

What Are The Causes Of Low Self-Esteem?

Negative past experiences take up an important role in the development of low self-esteem. Some of the definite factors that increase the chances of a person to develop low self-esteem are:

- **Past experiences involving neglect, abuse, or punishment:** Early life experiences like neglect, abuse, punishment, or bullying form an essential part. All those children who tend to suffer from these kinds of experiences often tend to believe that they are worthless and bad. They also start thinking that they must deserve some punishment now and then.

- **Not being able to meet the expectations of others:** You might have the feeling that you are not capable or good enough as you failed to meet the expectations of someone else. It might also include the unrealistic expectations of your parents. However, you will have to note that this does not indicate that the expectations were balanced or fair in the very first place.

- **Not being able to meet the standards of the peer group:** Being a bit different from others or being the 'odd' one out at the time of adolescence, when your identity was taking shape, can easily and powerfully impact the level of your self-esteem.

- **Not getting enough affection, warmth, love, encouragement, or praise:** It is quite possible to develop a low level of self-esteem even without the presence of overt negative incidents or experiences. It might be developed from a deficit of the positive ones as well. Without the presence of enough reinforcement that we are special, good, or loved, there are chances that children might form this impression that they are not good at all.

What Are The Things That Allows Low Self-Esteem To Go On?

It has been found that CBT has always been very interested in all those things that keep a major problem going. It is mainly because if we can successfully work out all those things that keep a major problem going, we can easily treat that problem by intervening to interrupt the cycle of maintenance. Two proper treatment programs have gained popularity, in particular for low self-esteem. Melanie Fennell, a psychologist, developed a proper influential model for cognitive behavior of low self-esteem. According to that model, throughout the course of your life, you keep forming negative beliefs regarding yourself, which she termed as the 'bottom line.'

In simple terms, your bottom line is the description of yourself. It can be summarized as something of this sort – "I am completely worthless," or "I am of no use at all." Your bottom line always stays at its place, in a dormant state. However, it tends to get activated only in certain situations.

When it gets activated, the chances are high that you will start using some strategies for being safe:

- **Start speaking to yourself critically:** Often done with the intention to motivate yourself, more often, it just results in paralyzing you. As the end result, it reinforces the bottom line.

- **Setting up flexible rules regarding how you should be:** We all set ourselves some 'rules' for living which are mostly intended to safeguard or protect us from having the worst fears confirmed. The primary problem is that the rules are not flexible at all. So, it can be said that breaking the rules might lead to more amount of self-criticism.

- **Creating anxious predictions regarding what might happen:** If we fail to see ourselves as being capable or competent, then the whole world would feel filled with danger often. The anxious portion of your mind will try to provide some help by predicting the potential threats. However, it will only make you feel more incapable.

- **Safety strategies and avoidance:** If you tend to think that all your flaws might be exposed, then it actually makes some sense to try and avoid the same. However, you will not get any chance to develop the idea of how well you might have coped up with the threat.

According to Fennell, although all such safety strategies can actually make you feel good in some ways for the short-term, all of them indicate that your bottom line actually never changes. It also indicates that your level of self-esteem never improves.

When you have a solid sense of self-esteem, you will be able to direct your life along a proper path that will provide you with great levels of satisfaction and happiness. Whenever you have low self-esteem, you will turn out to be self-critical, frustrated, and fearful by your inabilities to live your life in a way that feels good truly. A low level of self-esteem often gets maintained by a cycle of negative nature that keeps us frustrated and stuck. However, the good news is that CBT can actually provide you with some great tools that can help you to get out of the cycle. It will allow you to move in the direction of creating a life where you will get the chance to feel good about the path you are traveling on and also about yourself.

Benefits Of CBT Treatment For Unhealthy Self-Esteem

There are several benefits of CBT for treating low self-esteem.

- You will be able to discover certain behaviors and thoughts that feed the negative cycle of your low self-esteem. It will also provide you with the chance to develop some idea of what can be done to turn all this around.

- You will learn about various situations that tend to trigger your patterns of negative thinking along with your behaviors. CBT will teach you how you can stop this from taking place in the future.

- Get some new ways of behaving and thinking that will allow you to break free from feeling negative or bad. You will be able to develop the required level of confidence to feel good about yourself as you start developing a life that you can fully enjoy.

- Learn different strategies that will allow you to deal with the various challenges in life with full confidence. It will permit you to enjoy the pleasures of life with comfort and ease.

- Discover the ways in which you can feel like the boss of your life unhampered with the effects of self-doubt.

Signs Of Low Self-Esteem

Here are some signs that will depict you are having low self-esteem and how CBT can help to address the issues.

Sign #1: Inner critic Prevents You From Being Happy

All of us have an inner critic or voice that either criticizes us when we make a mistake or spurs us to achieve all our goals. As you suffer from low self-esteem, it might feel like that your inner critic is so much entrenched that you are not even able to get some clear perspective on reality. The inner critic functions hard so that it can bring you down and also stop you from moving ahead of the negative experiences in your life with any extent of self-belief. For instance, you might have just secured the job of your dreams.

But the inner critic will try its best to make you feel that you do not deserve the opportunity and you are not even capable of holding the position.

Our inner critics get formed right during our childhood days. They are made up of all those experiences that we had with all the authority figures, along with our peers, as we grew older. Your teachers or parents might have told you that you are of no worth or might also have been bullied. All such factors can easily contribute to the formation of your inner critic and also structure the way you view yourself. It will determine the way you believe in all your abilities.

How Does CBT Help?

As you deal with low self-esteem and especially self-criticism, CBT can help you to examine how your behaviors, thoughts, and beliefs might be contributing to the perceptions that we hold about ourselves and also about the world around us. During the sessions of CBT, your therapist will thoroughly work with you in order to properly identify the negative patterns of your thoughts along with your behavior. He/she will be sharing various techniques based on evidence that can help you to silence the inner critic effectively.

Sign #2: You Keep Taking Things Personally

Whenever you suffer from low self-esteem, it is a common thing to feel that some negative events or even experiences were targeted specifically at you or might be in some way your fault. The belief of this nature might have some negative impact on the relationships of your life. It might also affect the ways in which you try to interact in social settings. For instance, a colleague or friend of yours might have made a silly joke about you. The intention was to have some fun; however, for you, it acted as a crushing reinforcement of the negative view of yourself. All of this might then cause you to continuously ruminate on that joke, even long after it was actually told. You might then try to view that statement, which was actually intended in a joking way, as the true reflection of yourself.

How Does CBT Help?

CBT or cognitive behavioral therapy teaches us that as we suffer from various issues like low self-esteem, we might often get stuck in a system of the irrational belief that only tends to hold us back. When we start taking things personally, we try to hold to a specific belief system that just puts us right at the center and is intended as a victim. In this case, CBT can provide you with the required help with a realistic approach to the issues or events. Your CBT therapist will try to encourage you to look out for facts that can support this very new approach in place of just relying on the previous system of belief. For instance, you might only believe that your romantic partner has become irritable and distant from you. Instead of just submitting to the belief that you are fault that your partner is like this or that your partner wants to break off the romantic relationship, your therapist will try to encourage you to find out other reasons for which your partner might be short-tempered. Perhaps they are only under extreme pressure at work or might be just feeling unwell.

Sign #3: You Put People Down Or Try To Judge Others

All of us have an individual in our minds that always try to judge others in a harsh way or are highly opinionated. It might also be a characteristic that you can recognize within yourself. If we are trying to deal with low self-esteem personally, criticizing other people harshly or judging others might be a proper sign of some deeper issue that we possess with all our insecurities. If you are feeling quite low about yourself, it might feel really good to disparage others who are around you or your close ones.

How Does CBT Help?

Cognitive behavioral therapy or CBT can help us to build our self-esteem by allowing us to properly identify the negative behaviors and thoughts that we have first. Your CBT therapist will keep working with you so that you can discover some of your limiting beliefs that you might have regarding your abilities or yourself. He/she will help you in developing rational and new beliefs regarding yourself. If you ever find yourself judging others around you in a harsh way, your therapist will start working with you in order to identify the source of all these negative feelings. You will be able to replace all the negative feelings with positive patterns of helpful thinking that will contribute to a better and enhanced view of the world around you and yourself eventually.

Chapter 5: CBT Techniques That Will Help You Combat Anxiety

Anxiety is regarded as a part of the response that you might have if you tend to suffer from OCD. It is because anxiety is a natural human response to unfamiliar situations or threats. But there is much more with anxiety than only being a part of OCD. If you tend to suffer from anxiety, you are most likely to have several panic attacks, be scared of certain events or issues, and also be unable to get all of them out of your head. Also, you might find yourself incapacitated regularly through the fear of what might happen. It is essential to properly differentiate between anxiety and OCD. OCD is a kind of obsessive response to severe anxiety. It is a way to control or even deal with the anxiety and fear that is created by a given situation. Anxiety can be regarded as fear in itself. The fear that comes with anxiety is more severe in nature, and you might be unable to deal with the same.

Without proper help, fear might turn out to be paralyzing and also reduce all the enjoyment of your life dramatically. Perhaps what is worst about suffering from anxiety is that you will be aware of the problem or issue all the time. You might also try to deal with the same but are unaware of what should be done as the first step. It might turn out to be a deliberating disorder as you are most likely to struggle in order to deal with daily issues. It is actually possible to be a recluse effectively as you are very much scared of trying out new things. The more you try to delay before receiving any proper treatment, the more difficult it will be for you to start with the treatment. You will take longer to recover if you keep delaying. One of the definite benefits of CBT is that it can help in dealing with anxiety very well. Generally, people suffering from anxiety starts showing proper improvement within nine to ten sessions.

Learning About Anxiety

A very important first step to overcome any kind of psychological issue is to learn in detail about it. It is often termed psychoeducation. Trying to learn about the problem will provide you with the comfort of getting to know that you are not alone, and other people have also found various useful strategies to win over the same. Also, doing so will let your friends and family know more about the problem that you are suffering from. There are people who have the notion that having a better understanding of all their problems can be regarded as a great step in the direction of recovery. Well, it is true in every possible sense. For instance, a person who is suffering from regular panic attacks can start the treatment by learning in detail about a panic attack.

While learning about panic attacks, he/she will come to know that it is a very uncomfortable experience; however, it is temporary and not at all dangerous. Whenever you opt for CBT to treat your anxiety, your therapist will start by explaining the issue in detail as the first step. It will only be for your own good if you can learn about the same on your own before going for your therapy. It will be speeding up the entire process with almost instant results.

Effectiveness Of CBT For Treating Anxiety

It has been found that CBT is very effective for any person who is suffering from anxiety. It is mainly because of the proactive approach to speedy recovery along with full involvement from both sides, from you and your therapist. As you do so, it makes sure that you get the best possible response. Every case of anxiety is unique in its own way. So, as you opt for CBT for treating your anxiety, you will be treated as a different person and not just another same case. Indeed, you can opt for medications to reduce your levels of anxiety. However, it will only be masking the symptoms without even dealing with the main underlying issues. Treatment of anxiety with the help of CBT puts into use several scenarios along with the discovery of emotional response. It also involves the adjustment of the response in order to create a better form of response, which can effectively lower the level of anxiety.

For instance, a sudden invitation to a party can result in the creation of three emotive responses:

- Great happiness that you have been called for the party. You will look ahead to a superb party along with great excitement for being able to meet new people.

- A very neutral response. You might not mind going to parties; however, you might just prefer to stay at home. Either way, you do not feel bothered and can leave it or take it.

- A great level of anxiety. From the very moment you get the invitation, you will feel anxious about the same. You might probably feel worried about making a fool out of yourself or just turning up and finding out that it was a fake invite. Even though a very small part of you would like the idea of attending the party, your anxiety and fear would prevent you from attending the party. You will end up missing out a great experience.

With the help of CBT, you will come to know why the third option is your natural response. After you have figured out the reason, you can easily retrain your mind. As a result, your natural response will turn out to be excitement. Indeed, it is not going to happen overnight; however, it is achievable. Along with attempting to alter the way you actually react to certain situations, your CBT therapist will also need you to face all your fears. No matter what makes you anxious, it is needed to be faced both in the real world and in the office of the therapist. It is not that easy. However, it is important to ensure that you learn to live with all your disorder. Your CBT therapist will aid you in the process by working up to the bigger fears you have gradually. For instance, if one of your primary fears is speaking up in public, you are not going to be alone. The steps below will help you to make sure that you achieve the eventual goal.

- Watch others speak up and also make some notes on them. By making notes, it does not mean taking notes of the material.

- Write a proper speech.

- Start practicing the speech you have structured in front of a camera or a mirror. You can play back the speech if you record it in your camera to see how good it sounds and looks.

- Practice the same in front of your friends and family. Try to ask back for constructive feedback. All of this can help you to improve the quality of your speech.

- Give a visit to the venue where you will give your speech. Also, do not forget to check the place where you will stand.

- Try to go to the venue quite early on the day of your speech. See the audience arriving and try to work out what will appeal to all of them. It can help in tailoring your speech according to your audience.

- While giving your speech, do not just rush with it. Take it slow with enough pauses in between. It will permit you to put together all your thoughts, the audience to take in the information, and also, you will be on track.

As you break something big into several small steps, you will be able to deal with a small piece of your fear at every stage of the journey. The ultimate stage will not seem that scary as you actually envisioned it. It can be regarded as a very important step towards dealing with your anxiety and fear. Your CBT therapist will aid you in working through various scenarios. He/she will start with all those that make you the least anxious. They will be slowly working up in the direction of the ones which tend to strike fear deep in your heart. You will also be learning several techniques of relaxation that can be put to use by you to bring all your feelings of anxiety and panic under control. Finally, your therapist will offer you various complementary therapies.

The purpose of all these therapies will be mainly to reduce the overall amount of stress that you are facing. It will also help you to achieve a proper state of emotional balance. Some of the most common complementary therapies include:

- **Exercise:** It is a great natural way of relieving stress. According to various research, thirty minutes of proper exercise complete four to five times a week can help in readily reducing your anxiety. Also, opting for aerobic exercise for about one hour will do no harm.

- **Relaxation techniques:** It also includes muscle relaxation and meditation that can help in relieving anxiety. It will also help in making you feel more relaxed.

- There are various other techniques in CBT that we will discuss in the next sections.

Strategies Of Relaxation

Learning various ways in which you can relax your body can turn out to be very helpful for therapy. Shallow breathing and muscle tension are related to anxiety and stress. So, it is quite essential to be aware of all such bodily sensations and also to practice all of them regularly so that you can relax. Two of the most common strategies that are used in CBT are progressive muscle relaxation and calm breathing. In progressive muscle relaxation, you will have to systematically tense and relax various muscle groups. In calm breathing, you will have to slow down breathing consciously. Along with several other skills, the more you practice these two relaxation strategies, the more quickly and effectively they will function. Some other strategies for relaxation include meditation, listening to slow music, massage, and yoga. It is essential to realize that the primary goal of relaxation is not to eliminate or avoid your anxiety. It is all about making the ride a bit easier for you so that you can handle the feelings properly.

Realistic Thinking

Managing emotions of negative nature effectively involves identification of all kinds of negative thinking, along with replacing the same with realistic and balanced thinking. Altering all your unhelpful thoughts to realistic or helpful thoughts is the primary thing to feel better as all your thoughts have some huge impact on how you feel. 'Realistic thinking' is all about seeing yourself, other people, along with the whole world in a fairly balanced way. You cannot be excessivley positive or negative. For instance:

Example #1-

Unrealistic/unhelpful thought: I always have the habit of screwing up things. I am a big loser. What exactly is wrong with me?

More balanced and realistic thought: Everyone in this world makes mistakes, and so do I. I am a human being, and it is quite natural. All that can be done on my part is give all that I have to properly get the overall situation fixed and also try to get some knowledge from the experience.

Example #2-

Unrealistic and unhelpful thought: I can never do the job as I feel very anxious. Why am I unable to keep my anxiety under control?

More balanced and realistic thought: It is absolutely normal and okay to have anxious feelings. It is not that harmful to be anxious at times, and it can never stop me from doing anything in life. I can still opt for the party while feeling anxious.

How To Achieve Realistic Thinking

Start by having an idea about what you are actually trying to tell yourself or even thinking in your mind. The majority of us are not even concerned about paying any kind of attention to how we think, even when we are affected by all our thoughts constantly. Giving close attention to all our thoughts might readily help in keeping proper record of the type of thoughts that we have typically. After you are aware of all your thoughts, just give some effort to identify all those thoughts or imagination of yours that tend to give you some bad feeling. Also, make sure you determine whether they are problematic or not, that needs to be faced.

 For instance, in case you start feeling sad while having thoughts about your grandfather, who is on death bed due to cancer, such a thought does not require to be opposed face to face as it is completely a natural thing to have sad feelings while thinking about all those whom you love suffering. However, if you start feeling sad when a friend of yours cancels some dinner plans, and you just start thinking that something must be surely wrong with you and no one is interested in you, this is actually problematic. Such thoughts are extreme and are not at all reality based. Try to give attention to all the sudden emotional shifts, regardless of how large or small it is. Whenever you find that you are getting distressed/upset, just question yourself, "What am I saying to myself right now?" or "What exactly is making me feel distressed or upset?"

 Start with an examination of all those thoughts to find out if they are unhelpful or unrealistic once you get used to identifying all the thoughts properly that results in emotions of negative nature. One of the main things that you will have to opt for is to find out whether you have fallen into the traps of thinking. Thinking traps are ways of looking at everything in a negative way.

You might also opt for asking various questions to yourself in order to throw a challenge to all your thoughts of negative. For example, "What are the pieces of evidence that can prove this thought is true?" or "Am I just confusing a possibility with a mere probability? It might be possible, but is it very likely?" Finally, after you are done with challenging all your negative thoughts and evaluation of the same in a more objective way, try your best to find some alternative thought that is of realistic and balanced nature. As you do so, it can readily help in lowering level of distress. Along with developing various realistic statements, you will have to try to develop a collection of statements which are of quick coping nature and easy-to-remember.

Also, it can be very helpful if you opt for writing down all your thoughts that are realistic or the helpful coping statements on a piece of paper. Keep this piece of paper with you so that it can remind you of all such statements whenever you feel anxious or distressed to think with a clear mind.

Facing Your Fears: Exposure

It is completely normal to avoid all those things that you fear as this reduces the level of anxiety for the short term. For instance, in case you are scared of enclosed tight places, such as an elevator, opting for the stairs in place of that will result in making you much less anxious. But avoidance will stop you from learning that all those things that you are scared of are mot that dangerous as it seems to you. So, in that case, opting for the stairs will prevent you from learning or getting the idea that nothing bad is going to take place if you opt for the elevator. In cognitive behavioral therapy, the overall process of facing fears is known as exposure. It is often regarded as an essential step to learn how to manage anxiety effectively. Exposure includes repeatedly and slowly getting into situations of fear until you can lower down your level of anxiety. You will have to begin with all those situations/events that tend to make you a bit anxious. You will keep working on the way to face all those things that make your the level of anxiety rise.

 The first step in this process is to make a proper list of all the places, situations, or objects you are scared of. For instance, in case you are really scared of spiders while willing to win over the fear so that you get the chance to opt for camping along with all your friends, the to-do-list might include: seeing images of spiders, observing a spider either in an aquarium or at a zoo, watching videos of spiders, along with standing across a room from a person who is having a spider on his/her hand. After you successfully create a to-do-list, try to arrange the same from the ones that are least scary, while increasing the scare meter as you go up. Beginning with a event that makes you the least anxious, continuously being a part of that situation, or just facing that situation until you start feeling less anxious about the same, just keep up with it.

 After you are able to properly face that very event a number of times without anxiety of any kind, you can progress to the next big step on the prepared list. The therapy aims at stressing the essential need of facing all your fears regularly. The more someone involves in the practice, the faster all their fears will start fading. Having great wins, while also feeling great about the same can act as a superb motivator that will keep you going.

How Can You Prevent A Relapse?

Management of all your problems effectively is more or less like workout – you will have to be in proper shape, along with practicing all the useful skills as a regular habit. But at times, individuals just tend to get back to all their past habits, losing all kinds of progress or enhancements that they made so far. They just end up having a relapse. Having a relapse is nothing but a total return to all the past ways in which you used behave and think before you actually learned some new strategies to manage all your problems. Although it is quite normal for people to experience relapses at the time of low mood, fatigue, or extreme stress, a potential relapse is not necessary to take place. Let's have a look at some of the tips that can help you to prevent relapses and lapses of any kind.

- Continue with your skills of CBT. Keep practicing them as it is regarded as the perfect and the best way to prevent relapses. If you have the habit of practicing the skills regularly, you will learn to be in good shape to properly handle any kind of situation that you face in life. You can opt for making a routine for yourself for all those skills that you want to work upon each week.

- Try to be aware of the instances when you might be more vulnerable to experience a relapse. Try to figure out whether you can feel your old habits returning back at the time of stress or anxiety. Being aware of this will permit you to be less likely to experience one. Also, you might get some help to you create a recording of all the signs of warning such as frequent arguments with your close ones, more anxious thoughts, etc., that will indicate whether your anxiety level is increasing. Once you have figured out all your warning signs or the red flags, you will be able to make a plan of action so that you can cope with all of them. It might include, for instance, practicing some skills of CBT like challenging all your negative thoughts or calm breathing.

- Always remember that you are also working towards progress like all other people in this world. A great way to stop all your future relapses is to keep dealing with brand new challenges. The chances of sliding back to all your past habits will be very less in case you just keep your focus on new challenges.

- In case you already have experienced a lapse, give your best to find out all those events or situations that led your path to the same. It can provide you with the required help to make some plans so that you can cope with various types of situations in the coming days. Remember that it is absolutely natural to have lapses occasionally. Also, you will get the chance learn new things from your lapses.

- The way in which you think regarding your lapses has a great impact on future behavior. In case you keep thinking of yourself as a failure, along with just undoing all your dedicated works, you are most likely to just cease trying. You will result in having a relapse. In place of that, it is essential to remember that it is not at all possible to unlearn all those skills that you have learned and just return back to square one. It is because you have got all the ideas on how to take care of anxiety. In case you experience a relapse, you will be easily back on your usual track.

Chapter 6: CBT For Depression

Depressive disorder or rather depression belongs to the list of most common psychiatric disorders that can be found in various people today of any age across every region of the world. Although it might be present at any age, adolescence till early adulthood is the time between which it is the most common. Also, it has been found that depressive disorders affect females two times more than males. Depression can occur as various heterogeneous conditions in different types of clinical scenario that ranges from transient minor symptoms to debilitating and severe conditions that often results in severe occupational and social impairments. Generally, it gets presented with constellations of emotional, cognitive, physiological, behavioral, social, occupational, and interpersonal symptoms. The disorders can be of several severities, and a considerable proportion of the patients might turn out to have a recurrent illness. It is also highly present simultaneously with other medical conditions such as substance use, anxiety disorders, hypertension, diabetes, obsessive-compulsive disorder, and cardiovascular illnesses.

Evidence For Effectiveness Of CBT In Depression

CBT or cognitive behavioral therapy is often regarded as the best psychological intervention that is based on evidence for effective treatment of various psychiatric disorders. The uses of CBT have also been recently extended to behavioral medicine, psychotic disorders, stressful life situations, marital discord, and several other clinical conditions. Various detailed research has been conducted to show the efficacy of cognitive behavioral therapy for treating depressive disorders. A meta-analysis that included a total of 115 studies showed that CBT is a very effective strategy to be used as a treatment for depressive disorders. When combined with other treatments of pharmacotherapy, it works even better than pharmacotherapy alone. Also, it has been found that the rate of relapse of patients treated with CBT is quite less than all those patients who are treated with the help of pharmacotherapy alone.

Guidelines of treatment for depression suggest that psychological interventions are quite acceptable and effective to be used as a strategy for treating patients. Psychological interventions are generally used for depressive disorders that range between mild to moderate. Most of the therapists suggest CBT in place of other treatment options to treat depression, owing to its efficacy and quick resolution capabilities.

Contradictions For CBT

There are no definite contradictions to cognitive behavioral therapy. But it is often said that patients with severe comorbid disorders due to personalities such as subnormal intelligence and antisocial personality disorders are quite difficult to treat and managed with the help of CBT. Special expertise and training might be needed for treating all such patients. Also, patients who suffer from severe depression along with intentions of suicide and/or psychosis are tough to be managed with the help of CBT alone. Such patients might also need medications along with other types of treatments before opting for CBT.

However, there are various advantages of CBT in treating depression.

- It is used to lower down the symptoms of depression as a completely independent treatment or sometimes along with certain medications.

- It is effective in modifying the underlying beliefs or schemas that help in maintaining depression.

- It can be put into use to properly address several psychosocial problems such as job stress and marital discord, which can effectively contribute to the depressive symptoms.

- It can effectively reduce the overall chances of recurrence.

- Improves adherence to recommend other medical treatments.

Choice Of Treatment

Generally, CBT is performed on an OPD or outpatient department basis that includes various planned sessions. Each of the sessions lasts for about 50 minutes or one hour that depends on the suitability of both the parties – therapist and patient. In certain situations, CBT might also be delivered in inpatient settings that involve treatments as usual. For example, suicidal patients or patients with a high risk of self-harm, adjuvant treatment for severe depression, patients with various psychiatric or medical comorbidities, and also patients who are hospitalized for social reasons.

Use Of CBT Depending On Severity Of Depression

Several trials have effectively shown the various benefits of combined treatment for treating severe depression. Although a bit costlier than single therapy, combined therapy can provide you with the cost-effectiveness in the form of preventing relapses. The overall number of CBT sessions will depend on the responsiveness of the patient. Also, several booster sessions might be needed between the intervals of the first and twelfth month according to the clinical requirements.

Type of depression: Mild

Number of sessions: 7 – 12

Type of depression: Moderate
Number of sessions: 8 -16

Type of depression: Severe
Number of sessions: 16 or even more than that

Type of depression: Recurrent depression and chronic depression
Number of sessions: More than 16, along with booster sessions for one to two years

There is a general outline of CBT for treating depression:

- Mutual agreement on the definition of problems by patient and therapist

- Setting up goals

- Familiarizing and explaining patients with the CBT model

- Modification of behaviors and thoughts

- Application of new strategies and skills in sessions of therapy

- Prevention relapse

- Ending the therapy

Cognitive Depression Model

According to cognitive theory, people are not found to be influenced by life events. They tend to be influenced by the view that they have on the events. It indicates that individual differences in negative appraisal and maladaptive thinking processes of life events result in the development of various dysfunctional cognitive reactions. Such types of cognitive dysfunctions, in turn, are responsible for the other symptoms in behavioral and affective domains.

- Schema or stable kind of internal structure of information that is usually formed at the time of early life that also involves core belief regarding oneself.

- Intermediate beliefs and information processing are generally interpreted as the rules of living. They are usually expressed as "if and then" sentences.

- Automatic thoughts that are related proximally to daily events. In depression, it often reflects the cognitive triad, which is the negative view of the world, oneself, and the future.

The negative cognitive triad for depression is as follows:

- Helplessness – I am helpless.

- Hopelessness – The future is blank.

- Worthlessness – I am absolutely worthless.

Choice Of The Patient

There are several patient-related factors that can effectively facilitate the response to the treatment. Let's have a look at them.

- The primary thing that comes under consideration is the psychological mindedness of the concerned patient. All those patients who can easily understand and also label their emotions and feelings usually respond in a better way to CBT. Also, there are patients who tend to learn all those skills during the course of the treatment.

- The level of intellectualness of the patients can also affect the complete effectiveness of the therapy.

- Another great factor that comes into play is the motivation and willingness on the part of the patient. Indeed, it is not a prerequisite. However, all those who are motivated enough to properly analyze all their feelings and are ready to opt for various homework always show some better response to the overall therapy.

- The preference of the patient is the most primary factor. After the first assessment of the patient, who needs and prefers psychological treatment can be provided with CBT all alone or combining the same with other treatments relying on the depression type.

- All those patients who tend to suffer from mild to moderate depression can be provided with the first line of treatment.

- All those patients who suffer from severe depression might require a combination of both medications and CBT.

- Special consideration is needed in special situations—for instance, adolescents and children, lactation, pregnancy, medical comorbidities, etc.

Clinical Interview For CBT

Symptoms And Related Cognitions

Automatic negative thoughts can easily trigger and enhance the symptoms of depression. It might turn out to be very helpful to properly identify all the unhealthy automatic thoughts that are linked with the several symptoms of depression. Some of the most common symptoms, along with automatic thoughts, are:

- **Symptom:** Behavioral

  Automatic thoughts: It can't do this. It is excessive for me.

- **Symptom:** Guilt

  Automatic thought: I am only letting everyone down.

- **Symptom:** Shame

  Automatic thought: What does everyone think about me?

Coping Strategies And Impact On Functioning

It is essential to properly know the effect along with the extent of depression on interpersonal relationships and overall functioning. Sometimes patients might also opt for certain coping strategies that can actually make them feel good for a very short time, such as consumption of alcohol. However, in the long term, such coping strategies might turn out to be very harmful.

The first interview of the treatment comes with four general objectives:

- To develop a warm and collaborative therapeutic alliance

- To properly list certain problem set along with the associated goals

- To properly educate the patient about the cognitive model along with the vicious cycle that sustains the depression

- Providing the patient a proper idea about future treatment procedures.

The overall functioning of CBT can be explained in all these headings:

- Starting the treatment

- Behavioral interventions

- Working on the negative automatic thoughts

- Ending the session

- Starting Treatment

The treatment is started with gaining proper knowledge about the problems of the patient, along with letting the patient know about the procedures that will be followed. These can actually convey two messages – a) It is actually possible to make sense of persisting depression; b) There is something very important that can be done by the patient about it. All these messages can directly address helplessness and hopelessness.

- **Identification of goals and problems:** The several types of problems that are faced by the patient need to be included in a proper list, which can also include the symptoms of social problems or depression. The development of such a list right at the end of the very first session can help in establishing the goals of the treatment.

- **Introduction of cognitive depression model:** During the first session, it is important to get a basic idea about how the cognitions affect the behavior and emotions of the patient. The data that is provided by the patient can be helpful to give proper insight into the behaviors.

- **Where to start from:** The common goal of the treatment is agreed upon by the therapist and the patient. Thus, it can be said that a therapeutic alliance is very important in CBT.

Behavioral Interventions

Reduction of ruminations: It has been found that all those patients who suffer from depression tend to spend a great amount of time focusing all their attention on all their shortcomings. Making patients aware of all such negative ruminations and diverting their attention consciously towards some of the positive aspects can help in speeding up the process.

Monitoring the activities: Loss of interest in daily activities is a sure sign of depression. It has been found from various research that behavioral interventions can easily increase the autonomy sense in patients. If you opt for CBT to get rid of depression, you will be taught to record all your activities hour by hour on your activity schedule. Each of your activities will have to be rated between 0 – 10 for pleasure (P) and (M) for mastery. The rating 'P' will indicate how enjoyable your activity was, and the 'M' rating will indicate how much of the activity you have achieved. Most of the depressed patients tend to feel low on their achievements the majority of the time. So, 'M' can be explained as "achievement that you felt while doing the activity." You will have to rate your activities immediately and not at all retrospectively.

Planning Activities

Once the patient learns to monitor himself/herself, activities for each day are planned. It helps patients by:

- Providing a structure and also helps in setting up priorities.

- Avoiding the requirement to keep making important decisions regarding what to do next.

- Changing perception from all types of chaos to manageable jobs or tasks.

- Increasing the chances that all the activities will be performed.

- Enhancing the sense of control of the patient.

A proper plan for activities is structured in such a way that both mastery and pleasure are extensively balanced, for example, listening to music followed by ironing clothes. All those tasks that are most of the time avoided by the patient can be easily divided into several graded tasks. The patient is taught to properly evaluate every day in extensive detail and is also encouraged to keep a record of all their negative, unhelpful thoughts regarding their tasks. Some of the other important behavioral activities include:

- **Mindfulness meditation:** It helps people to stay grounded in the current situation by staying away from all types of ruminations.

- **Visualization:** It helps people stay motivated by visualizing the best part or the rewarding part of the day.

- **Successive approximation:** Breading down larger jobs/tasks into several smaller tasks that can be accomplished easily.

- **Pleasant activity scheduling:** Planning all those activities that are pleasant in nature during the course of the day.

Identification Of Negative Automatic Thoughts

Patients learn various ways to record all types of upsetting incidents right after they opt for therapy. They learn:

- To identify all the unpleasant emotions, such as anger, guilt, despair, etc., along with the signs that can depict negative thinking is already present. The emotions are rated for their intensity on a scale of 0 – 100. All these rating help in making several small changes in their emotional state when their search for alternatives to all their negative thoughts starts. It is very important as change is all-or-nothing rarely, and all the small improvements might be missed otherwise.

- To identify the situation of the problem. What was the concerned patient thinking about or doing when a painful emotion emerged? For instance, "waiting for hours at the checkout of the supermarket" or "continuously worrying about by better half returning home late."

- To identify negative thoughts that are associated with all types of unpleasant emotions. Your therapist might ask, "What went through your mind right at that moment?" In such instances, patients tend to become aware of all their images, thoughts, or implicit meanings that are persistent when emotional shifts record and occur. Belief in every thought is rated on a scale of 0% - 100%.

Questioning The Negative Thoughts

Your therapist will help you to figure out all the dysfunctional automatic thoughts with the help of "guided discovery."

- What is the evidence?

- What are the alternative views?

- What are the probable advantages and disadvantages of thinking in this way?

- What are the biases of thinking?

Common Cognitive Distortions

- **Black and white:** Situations always viewed in two categories only in place of a continuum. For instance, "If I cannot top my exams, I will be a failure."

- **Fortune telling:** Future is generally predicted in a negative way without even considering other types of possible or the more likely outcomes. For instance, "I will be upset that I cannot even function at all."

- **Discounting or disqualifying the positive:** Telling oneself unreasonably that all the positive deeds, experiences, or qualities do not even count. For instance, "I successfully cracked the exam, but that does not indicate I am a great being. It was all a fluke."

- **Emotional reasoning:** Thinking something has to be true as he/she feels it so strongly. The evidence is discounted or rather ignored. For instance, "I know it that I can successfully get done with all my tasks. But I still feel that I am incompetent."

- **Labeling:** Putting a global and fixed label on others and oneself without trying to consider that the available evidence might reasonably result in a less disastrous conclusion. For instance, "I am a failure, and he is not good enough too."

- **Minimization or magnification:** Evaluating oneself, someone else, or a situation, and magnifying the negative and/or minimizing the positive unreasonably. For instance, "Scoring C grade in exams shows how poor I am in studies. Also, scoring high marks would not mean that I am smart."

- **Selective abstraction:** Paying undue attention to all the negative details of oneself without looking at the whole picture. For instance, "As I only scored passing marks in my exams, it indicates that I am a bad student."

- **Overgeneralization:** Making a negative conclusion that tends to go far beyond the present situation. For instance, "As I felt uneasy at the meeting, I do not possess all those things needed to be a leader."

- **Mind reading:** Believing that oneself knows what other people are thinking without considering other possibilities. For instance, "He thinks that his boss assumes him as a novice for this task."

- **Personalization:** Believing that other people are behaving in a negative way because of him/her, without trying to find out other explanations for their respective behavior. For instance, "The guard did not smile at me as I might have done something wrong."

- **Tunnel vision:** Viewing only the negative aspects of any situation. For instance, "My colleague cannot do any task right. He is casual, insensitive, and callous towards his duties."

Ending The Treatment

CBT is a kind of therapy that is time-limited and goal-directed as well. So, the patients are generally made aware of the end of the treatment in advance. It can be done in the following stages:

- Identification of dysfunctional assumptions

- Consolidation of learning blueprint

- Preparation for setback

Chapter 7: Changing Core Beliefs With CBT

Core beliefs are deep-seated assumptions that tend to guide all our behaviors. It also affects the way we see ourselves and also try to perceive various situations. All such beliefs impact how we feel, the way we relate to other people, along with guide our satisfaction, success with relationships and life. Core beliefs are believed to be 'core' to the identities. All of them might feel deeply interweaved, just like our name and gender. You won't feel good or right in case you ever have the thought of getting a new name. The similar thing applies to your self-belief. All of us have worn all of our beliefs for such a long time that getting some new set of beliefs does not just feel good/right. So, it takes some time to get changed or altered.

The core-beliefs just feel similar to truths. They might also turn out to be quite challenging to change. They are the ones who are generally responsible for all our self-doubt, continual insecurity, continuous desire for external approval or validation, and low moods. They can easily push us in the direction of ineffective behavioral patterns like perfectionism or people-pleasing. We also have the habit of noticing situations and events that tend to confirm the beliefs that we have in core and move our eyes away from all those that just go in the opposite direction all the core beliefs. Self-belief can be regarded as the 'inner walls' that do not have any form of doors. They just prevent us from getting to experience some different possibilities in our lives. Also, it is essential to keep a note that our core beliefs are not facts.

How Do Our Core Beliefs Tend To Develop?

Our beliefs are similar to all our thoughts that we try to affirm to ourselves continuously. We also which believe them to be the only truth. A belief might include some simple kind of thought like "My life is very hard," or it might also include some tough range of thoughts and statements such that exist in a belief system. No matter you actually have the knowledge of the same or not, you will continuously affirm all those things that you believe. Also, if you ever listen to your own self truly, you will be able to make a case regarding the 'correctness' of all the beliefs continually. It might happen even in cases when all the concerned beliefs tend to be quite harmful for your well-being and happiness. The 'lawyer' inside you will continuously try to justify and be 'correct' while trying to make all remaining beliefs to be 'wrong.' The way in which a system of belief is maintained is to continuously affirm it, along with justifying the same without any kind of questions.

Core Beliefs Can Impact The Life Happiness

All of us have developed some of our core beliefs in all sectors of lives. All such beliefs can effectively impact the success, happiness, along with personal fulfillment. People develop core beliefs in order to understand and just sustain in the world that surrounds them.

Beliefs Are Similar To Our Thoughts

Our core beliefs are our thoughts that we assume to be true over time. But they are sometimes developed on the basis of the early experiences in life. It might not point out what is really 'true' for many individuals do. They might turn out to be quite strong forces that can shape all our perceptions as they seem to be true, along with being so real. They might even feel very difficult to be changed.

Core Beliefs Can Push Us In The Direction Of Negative Automatic Thoughts

It is a proper example from the process of CBT of how our beliefs developed in past life can push us in the direction of negative self-talk in later life. The negative nature of self-talk will contribute to several not to helpful symptoms, along with behaviors. Self-talk of negative nature often includes various kinds of cognitive distortions. Let's have a look at how the overall cycle functions.

- **Early experiences:** Comparison to others or criticism

- **Unhelpful assumptions:** "I am below everyone else," "All my worth depends on what other people think of me."

- **Critical incident in life:** Breakup in relationships

- **Cognitive distortions or negative automatic thoughts:** "I will be staying alone forever," "It is all because of me," "Something is definitely wrong with me."

- **Symptoms:** Motivational, self-criticism, loss of interest, behavioral, procrastination, sadness, guilt, poor concentration, social withdrawal, anxiety, , indecisiveness, feelings, loss of appetite, loss of sleep.

Examples Of Development Of Core Beliefs

Let us assume that you used to share all your emotions and feelings with your parents as a child. Your parents kept telling you that you were incorrect or 'wrong' all the time. Perhaps they might have done so in a properly meaning way. In case you have said, "I do not get the feeling of fitting in, and I think other kids hate me," your parents might not have wanted that you develop this kind of negative thoughts. They must have said, "You are not right, and what you are thinking or feeling is not true at all." When this tends to happen continuously with every negative kind of emotion that you get to know in life, with time, you might build the belief that you are always incorrect. Slowly, you will not be able to have faith in yourself, and you might not even be able to trust in all your emotional signs. In case you tend to believe that you are always incorrect at a fundamental level, you will find it quite tough to start expressing your thoughts in an assertive way. You will find it daunting to feel worthy, trust yourself, or just feel that you are deserving.

Such beliefs will slowly drive many types of life aspects. If in case, you were mistreated in your childhood by adults, you might form a belief, "I am not safe at all." During childhood, it makes complete sense to end up in this kind of conclusion. Also, it will protect you from having trust on other adults who might have the intention of mistreating you. But when you grow up to be an adult, belief of this nature might stop you from developing new links, along with having trust on others. In actuality, the overall fact might realistically have been, "I cannot trust mother/father to take proper care of my needs or to protect me."

Why Is It Important To Uncover All Your Core Beliefs?

If you just ever feel that you are stuck in a pattern that keeps repeating, perceptions and feelings of others, or a behavior that you really want to change, you are most likely to possess a core belief that helps run the overall game. For instance, in case you possess some core belief, "The world is not at all safe, and I cannot really trust other people," the chances are high that you might feel anxious or just face difficulties in maintaining or forming new relationships. You might also have behaviors or habits that might turn out to be exhausting at times, such as obsessive thinking, poor boundaries, perfectionism, or compulsive behaviors. Now, as you might imagine, you might not be able to figure out the link that lies between any deep embedded belief that your surrounding or the world is not at all secure and your anxiety. All that you can notice is that you are anxious.

It can help in developing the connection that exists between all the beliefs and the way you feel about them. It will provide you with the very chance to move one step back, while having a look at the whole picture in a completely other way. You will get some chances to face the belief and also make yourself aware that you are absolutely safe at this moment. It will help you to move all ther focus from your anxiety to all those actions required to be opted for and get available at the current situation.

Negative Nature Of Core Belief Might Result In Self-Sabotage

Let us assume that you are trying to work hard in the direction of a dream job that you always wanted. But you find out that as you start moving forward in the direction of your goal, you discover yourself self-sabotaging all the successes, feeling anxious, avoiding all those things you actually require to do, and procrastinating. You might also start wondering, "What exactly is wrong with me? What is the reason that I keep stalling all the time? I want to achieve this goal so bad!" However, what you might fail to understand is that you are holding a heavy belief that success is not meant for you, other people might figure out that you are fake, or getting success in life will need you to handle more than your capabilities.

Again, all of these are not at all thoughts that we tend to be aware of on a regular basis. What you can suddenly notice at the time of trying to work on the career dream is, "I just need to take a short break," "Maybe I need to update my resume once again." You are not trying to think, "I am not worthy at all" or "I cannot ever have what I want in life." But this might turn out to be a belief that is trying to run the entire show. Successfully discovering all your beliefs will help in taking complete charge of your life. It will also help to identify the unconscious forces that tend to drive all our behaviors, along with thoughts, which motivates us to try or opt for something new or variable. The ultimate goal is to alter all the beliefs, followed by changing your life.

How Can CBT Help In Changing Core Beliefs

Core beliefs might turn out to be quite challenging to be altered or changed as most of the time; they are automatic beliefs that are hidden and have also turned out to be a natural part of all our overall identities. Getting knowledge about how to challenge, identify, and also reframe all the self-defeating thought along with your core belief is a very essential step in improving your health of your emotions. CBT or cognitive behavioral therapy comes with various steps that can help you to properly discover and then change the core beliefs. CBT involves a very straightforward method that helps in throwing a challenge to your core beliefs.

- The process starts with the identification of your beliefs that you always believed to be true. Your therapist will provide you with a core belief worksheet that will help you identify all those beliefs that seem quite familiar.

- Asking yourself, "Will it benefit in any way if I try to maintain and preserve this specific belief? Is this particular belief really valid and true? What are the possible advantages/disadvantages of believing this belief?"

- Reversing the beliefs or considering in case the exact reverse belief might turn out to be true as well. For instance, "I must try to hide all my true feelings." You can try to reverse the same by uttering to yourself, "It is absolutely okay to express all my true feelings" or "I must try to control my partner" to "I should try to accept my partner." You can opt for various other ways in which you can effectively change the direction of your beliefs or bring uprfront the opposite. Just keep playing in several ways and then ask yourself to reverse the same and find out whether the opposite could be more helpful or true than the original one.

Technique Of What-If Downward Arrow For All Your Anxiety Beliefs

A very widely used technique might be effectively put to use to deal with your anxiety beliefs – the what-if downward arrow technique. Its purpose is to properly identify all those things that you are actually scared of. What exactly is the deep-seated catastrophe/fear that you are always trying to stay away from? You might regard all the core beliefs as the core fears. You will have to follow these steps:

- Discover a proper automatic thought of negative nature.

- Ask yourself, "What if all those thoughts were true? What are the worst things that could possibly happen? What am I most scared of?"

- Continue writing the following thought that develops in your mind and keep asking the same questions by redoing the overall cycle till the time you can reach the base of all the anxieties, worries, or tension. If you tend to face any problem in any of these steps, your CBT therapist will always be there to help you out.

- After you have successfully figured out the 'worst' fear, again ask yourself, "How likely this might happen?" or "Can I live with the same if it did happen?"You will have to find out any other underlying emotions that you think might contribute to the fear.

Chapter 8: Work Through Procrastination With CBT

Pablo Picasso said, "Only try to put off until the next day what you are truly willing to die having them left undone." I am not sure about you all, but this quite is something that can get me moving. CBT for procrastination is the answer that you require if you are willing to get out of all your procrastination habits. You will get to know about the two important CBT components, how they work, what the overall process of CBT for procrastination involves, and various other things you need to get going in this chapter.

At times, all of us are guilty of putting certain things off. It does not even matter whether it is about paying your taxes, organizing the closet, finishing an important file, or as simple as going to the gym. Whatever it is that we all are guilty of putting off, don't you feel all the time like it is not the 'perfect' time? We just keep waiting for the 'perfect' moment, to get some more energy, the best opportunity, or even to be in the perfect state of mind. However, the 'perfect' time never comes, and we just end up doing nothing at all. Right then, before we are even aware of it, we just find ourselves running behind everyone else, upset, defeated, and overwhelmed. Now, all those things that seemed not a possible lot much long ago are quickly getting out of reach. Can you properly relate?

All you are doing is procrastinating about certain sectors of your life. As we procrastinate, it will prevent us from performing all those tasks that we should be doing for our own good. For instance, you have got some serious presentation to be submitted within five days at your workplace. You just waste the first four days researching without even starting with the presentation. You have got all your needs, but still, you feel you need more, and this is not the perfect moment to start the job. You end up missing the deadline where the villain is your procrastination habit. What are the life areas that you are procrastinating about? No matter what it is, there is nothing to feel ashamed about. The roadblock of procrastination is quite common in all our lives.

It turns out to be problematic only when it takes up the chronic shape, reduces life quality, or just impairs all our performance. So, what are the possible ways in which we can un-stuck our lives and ourselves? How can we possibly overcome the trap of procrastination? One of the most effective options of treatment is CBT or cognitive behavioral therap. You can also call it procrastination CBT.

Primary Components Of CBT

In the field of psychotherapy, procrastination CBT consists of two main components. They are behavioral and cognitive.

Cognitive

Cognitively indicates your processes of thinking like beliefs, attitudes, along with ideas. The cognitive aspect that is linked to the problem of procrastination is quite known. Therapists who deal with the cognitive aspect often refer to procrastination as continuously looking out for some nature of justification to delay all jobs or tasks. All those who procrastinate also have the tendency to describe the dysfunctional thinking as all the conditions will turn out to be better after some time. It is all about these nature of cognitive processes that underpin the way in which procrastination can provide us with the optimism of false nature that everything might turn out to be 'right' enough eventually to tackle all forms of activities. So, to alter a cognitive aspect of this sort, you will have to alter the way in which you try to organize all your thinking. One of the definite ways in which this can be done is by identifying your inner critic voice and then try to opt for the exact opposite that is being told by your inner critic.

Behavioral

According to this nature of therapy, all our behaviors can be learned. So, it can be said that behaviors can be altered with time. The main aim of behavioral therapy is to properly get to know specific patterns of behavior that tend to cause several problems within a person. It then tries to examine the disempowering and harmful behaviors that you try to opt for. It also figures out ways to help you learn about why all of them occur. In true sense, therapy of this form aims at developing new ways to quell all your behaviors before it actually starts.

It is quite essential to keep a note that CBT does not make the problem vanish or go away just like that. Rather, it will help you to properly manage all of the problems positively. Also, it will encourage you to reexamine all the actions and the way they might affect how you feel and think. In place of just concentrating on the main causes of your symptoms or distress in the past, the process of procrastination CBT will find out ways in which the overall state of your mind can be improved.

How Does Procrastination CBT Work?

CBT or cognitive behavioral therapy functions by altering your beliefs, thinking patterns, along with your behavioral habits. One of the primary beliefs of CBT is that the thinking pattern of distorted nature can result in troublesome behaviors and distress. Some of the most common causes related to distorted thinking pattern are: focusing on the negative, overgeneralizing, along with catastrophizing. If all the thoughts are extremely negative or most of the time not positive, it can easily prevent you from doing things or viewing all those things that tend to disconfirm all those things that you actually believe to be true. In simple terms, all that you do is to just keep holding on to the similar nature of thoughts of disempowering nature along with beliefs. You just fail to get knowledge of something new. The steps of CBT for dealing with procrastination target to address all such problems by altering your thinking patterns, behavioral habits, and beliefs.

It will encourage you to think in a realistic way with no form of negativity, which permits you to properly respond in an effective way to challenge all the circumstances of your life. It also functions by providing you with the required help to stay away from patterns of negative thoughts and behaviors for achieving a healthier outlook. One of the approaches used by CBT to bring about change is to put into the picture some new ways of reacting. It helps in breaking out of the negative cycles quite quickly. For example, CBT will encourage you to get knowledge from all your mistakes and just move on in place of just thinking that you are nothing but a complete failure as you just continue procrastinating regarding completing your tasks or jobs. You will feel more confident and energized you with the help to feel more confident and energized with the new way of thinking and then reacting. The overall process often starts with clear identification of the problem, which is then followed by the establishment of some attainable goals, empathic communication, frequent feedback, reality checks, along with using some learned nature of tools to develop positive growth and behavior.

What Does The Overall Process Of CBT Involve?

You can opt for CBT in cooperation with your therapist in one-to-on or in a proper group discussion setting. The first option of CBT generally involves various sessions of therapy. CBT will generally include the process as follows, which is the similar kind of process used by therapists in order to treat extreme procrastinating cases.

- The therapist will start with breaking down the problem of procrastination into various portions during the sessions of therapy. All these areas consist of your emotions, thoughts, actions, and physical nature of feelings.

- In the next step, you will analyze all these portions so that you can work on them to find out whether they are unhelpful or unrealistic for which your CBT therapist will help. They will also provide you with the required help to discover any of your underlying thoughts, behaviors, along with beliefs all of which are resulting in your distress.

- The next step is to work to determine the overall effect that all of the areas have on you.

- Gradually, you will start working out the way you can alter the unhelpful, unrealistic, disempowering behaviors, along with thoughts. This will change the way you actually feel regarding all your problems of procrastination as the final result. It will also permit you to alter your behavior in a better way and control all your thoughts in the coming time.

The Best Techniques Of CBT To Deal With Procrastination

There are various techniques of CBT that can be used to overcome your problems of procrastination. Let's have a look at some of them.

Behavioral Activation

It helps a person to change any ongoing pattern of procrastination so that all the commitments and tasks can be approached properly in place of just being avoided. It generally needs some type of exposure of graded nature while taking into consideration the very fact that problem of procrastination gets reinforced by not willing to experience any kind of discomfort. Behavioral activation also provides great help in changing the way you actually think regarding all your tasks by paying attention to your expectations, the kind of person you are, along with your values. Together with the help of CBT therapist, you will be able to easily assess where all these actually 'fit' in how you are trying to handle all your jobs/tasks. The working patterns will surely differ from one individual to the other. So, it is quite essential to keep in mind that the outcomes you desire will also vary from the desired outcomes of others.

Behavioral Experiments

CBT therapists opt for experiments of behaviors to properly evaluate the working methods along with the presumptions related to your own capability to attain or reach certain goals. Clients will put into use the aspects of their behavior that tend to stimulate them to enjoy some activities. It will also help to adopt some mastery sense over any task, which directly provides in the significant reduction of procrastination. One of the ways in which this can be accomplished is by opting for the use of coping cards. You will have to write your strategy of coping up or your plan on a small card. You will have to keep the card with you and use the same to effectively overcome any kind of procrastination at your work.

Mindfulness Training

Mindfulness training is a very effective CBT technique for dealing with procrastination that concentrates on awareness of feelings and thoughts without any kind of judgment or attachment. While procrastinating, we tend to get entangled in all our thoughts regarding that situation, which just makes the way we actually feel worse. Practicing effective mindfulness helps in short-circuiting the overall technique by providing patients with the needed help to free ourselves from all their patterns of distorted thinking. It will help them to connect with the actual situation. It will enable us to address the tough tasks more skillfully and to do so with much less psychological sufferings and emotional reactivity.

Exposure Therapy

With the help of this CBT technique, procrastination can be easily dealt with in no time at all. It is a very powerful method to help you overcome all your anxieties. It includes exposing the concerned individual to any situation that results in anxiety. However, it is done only to a certain point at which the concerned person can keep their anxiety under control. For effective working of the therapy, the person will have to stay in that situation for a longer period of time until their level of anxiety decreases. Once this starts happening, the person is then put forward or presented to a tougher situation. The process keeps going on until the concerned person can tackle all the tasks and situations that they desire to conquer. For example, you can start using an alarm on your mobile phone or an egg timer to effectively set a specific portion of time to complete a task.

The whole strategy of CBT can be very helpful if you are that kind of person who can easily spend half an hour editing a document for which a maximum of fifteen minutes would be enough. The feeling of trying to work in opposition to a fixed deadline can easily enhance the efforts to move you in the very direction of completing the task.

Voice Training

Some of the recent findings related to CBT for procrastination related to voice training have shown some great improvements in the general distress and well-being of an individual. The voice or voices in this very therapy are all those that tend to externalize the worries of an individual and also distress the experiences of that person. Therefore, voice training therapy focuses on silencing the deep-seated inner critic. It also helps in putting the tension outside the boundary of you. You will have to go through five proper steps.

- **Awareness:** What is the voice trying to tell you?

- **Analysis:** What is the type of relationship that is present between your emotions and the messages of the voice?

- **Interrogation:** What are all those beliefs that are present right below the messages of the voice?

- **Fighting:** Changing all the lies or voice messages to reality or truth.

- **Maintenance:** Proper management of relapse.

Controlling Stimulus

CBT therapists often use the term stimulus control in order to dissect situations in which some types of behaviors might get triggered by the absence or presence of a certain stimulus. If you have coffee while working in front of your laptop, it can possibly indicate that your habit of drinking coffee gets controlled by the very stimulus of working in front of your laptop, for instance. You can easily learn how to maximize your motivation to take the required actions by controlling all the environmental cues that tend to direct us either in the direction of procrastination or work. There are two proper ways in which this can be done with stimulus control.

- **Unplugging from all types of
distractions:** In this age and day, it is
quite easy to get away your attention with
the wide collection of tech products that
are present around us. Silence your
phone, stay away your social media, turn
off the TV, and look for some productive
place where you can get done with all your
work if there is something that requires
your attention. Try to opt for some breaks.
You can also reward yourself between
your work sessions. The most essential
thing is to have the capability to identify
that you can also concentrate on being
productive for a longer time.

- **Rewarding for all the positive
steps:** Try to give yourself some reward
when you successfully complete a difficult
job or at least a portion of the job. You can
get some alone time so that you can get
the opportunity to opt for some things of
nonsensical nature that you actually
enjoy. Linking your work completion with
all the positive activities eventually is the
primary aim. So, you will be getting done
with all your tasks as a positive activity
within itself. The reward/gift comes in the
picture right after completion, similar to
the tasty dessert that gets introduced after
finishing your boring broccoli.

Chapter 9: CBT For Anger Management

Anger is a very natural and common human response that, when expressed in the proper way, can result in various kinds of effective constructive changes and coping strategies. If left unmanaged, anger might also get out of control and result in problems both in your personal and professional lives. Also, it comes with the capability of affecting important life areas of others. Anger acts as a very powerful kind of emotion that can easily trigger the 'fight or flight' response of the body. When your level of anger reaches a certain level, your body will change biologically while releasing stress hormones to provide you with the required help to deal with the stressful event. An adrenaline rush of this kind might feel empowering temporarily, along with stress-relieving. However, it comes with the power to put the body under immense pressure and also uses up a great deal of energy.

The continuous flow of the stress hormones can lead to harm to various systems of your body eventually. Both suppressed and explosive anger can push you towards a greater risk of having a heart attack, high blood pressure, depression, anxiety, and stroke. CBT can help you in properly managing your anger by making you understand the anger. It will also provide you with various ways in which you can express your anger.

What Is Anger And Why It Is Needed?

The function of all our emotions is to effectively communicate to ourselves, along with others, and also to motivate all our behaviors. Anger is an automatic, natural response that gets developed to unfairness either to someone, or ourselves, or something that we actually care about. It provides us with the required help to be alert of wrong decisions or wrongdoings. It also provides us with the energy to make everything right. It is a kind of emotion that can range from low irritability to super intense range. Anger is a feeling that often gets accompanied by various biological changes like enhanced heart rate, energy, testosterone, and blood pressure. All such changes might also make you shake, get sweaty and hot, and also feel like losing all control. Anger is, most of the time, seen as a very negative emotion. But it also comes with various positive functions:

- It can motivate us to make some important changes in life.

- It can help in resolving interpersonal conflicts.

- It helps in the promotion of self-esteem.

- It can help us by providing insight into ourselves.

- If aimed at a solution and justifiable, it can help and strengthen relationships.

Signs That Your Anger Might Be A Problem

Anger is not wrong all the time. Losing your cool occasionally does not indicate that you have some problem. Anger acts like a normal response to injustice and mistreatment. However, it might turn out to be a problem if it creates problems for others. Some of the signs that your anger might be a problem:

- Your anger involves uncontrolled acts of violence, rage, or outbursts

- You get angry most of the time

- You start thinking that your anger is the only way for being heard

- Your anger creates problems in your relationships

- You are getting depressed or anxious about your anger

- Your anger is resulting in self-harm

How Can CBT Help In Managing Anger?

CBT is a kind of psychotherapy that lasts for a very short span of time. It needs proper cooperation from the side of the patient to bring in the desired changes. It can be said that process of CBT is a collaborative approach to treating problems. CBT for managing your anger involves your CBT therapist to use a wide range of activities and questions that will help you identify and also understand the anger triggers. Your therapist will provide you with the required help to test all your beliefs and alter the same. The assumptions that you hold might also be tested to understand the hostility sequence. After you are aware of all your triggers along with the root causes of the same, you will be taught various strategies and skills to deal with your anger. Some of the skills include cognitive changes, assertive communication, relaxation, and problem-solving skills, and many more.

Anger is often regarded as an inevitable portion of life and is most of the time expressed in response to hurt, pain, or injustice. It is a learned response that can be unlearned with the help of CBT with a little bit of effort from your side. If you feel that your anger is making your life problematic, do not waste any time and opt for a CBT therapist.

Chapter 10: Treating Insomnia With CBT

Insomnia is a very common sleep disorder that can make it really hard to fall asleep, tough to stay asleep, or just make you wake up early and not being able to get back the sleep again. Effective treatment is quite hard to find in the case of insomnia. However, no matter what you try, never opt for any kind of drug that can help you in falling asleep. Cognitive behavioral therapy for insomnia, also termed as CBT-I, is a very effective treatment when it comes to chronic sleeping problems. Generally, it is recommended as the first option of treatment. CBT-I is a quite structured program that can help you identify and replace all your behaviors and thoughts that tend to worsen or cause sleep problems. It also helps in getting rid of all those habits that do not permit you to have a sound sleep. CBT-I can readily help in overcoming all the underlying problems that result in sleep disorder.

Living with insomnia can turn out to be a real challenge. Luckily, CBT-I can help you stay asleep, fall asleep faster, and also help to feel more rested during the course of the day. In order to find out how to treat your problems of insomnia, your therapist might want you to keep a sleep diary in detail for about one or two weeks.

How Does CBT-I Function?

CBT-I primarily concentrates on finding the overall link among the things we do, the way we sleep, along with the way we think. At the time of the treatment, a trained provider of CBT-I will help you to identify feelings, thoughts, and behaviors that tend to contribute to most of the problems of insomnia. Feelings and thoughts about sleep are tested and examined to find out whether they are correct, while the way you behave are tested and taken care of to find out whether they can promote sleep. Then your CBT-I instructor will try to clarify or even restructure the misconceptions along with the obstacles in a professional way. All of these can be more conducive for providing you with restful sleep. The overall treatment will take about six to eight sessions. However, the duration of the treatment might differ depending on the needs of the respective patients. The treatment can also be of two short sessions if provided by a doctor of primary care.

CBT-I is often referred to as a multicomponent treatment as it tends to combine various types of approaches in one. The sessions can include behavioral, educational, and cognitive components.

- **Behavioral interventions:** Stimulus control, relaxation training, along with sleep restriction helps to aid relaxation. It can help in establishing healthy habits of sleep.

- **Psychoeducational interventions:** Giving essential information regarding the link between feelings, thoughts, behaviors, and sleep is the main part of CBT-I.

- **Cognitive interventions:** It aims to alter unhelpful or inaccurate thoughts regarding sleep.

The flow and order of each of the components might vary depending on the approach of the provider, along with the unique needs of every person. Let us have a look at some of the most common techniques of CBT-I.

Cognitive Restructuring

In all those individuals who suffer from sleep problems, dysfunctional or inaccurate thoughts regarding sleep can result in various behavioral changes that might make sleep much harder than before, which, in turn, tends to reinforce all the thoughts of dysfunctional nature. For instance, past experiences related to insomnia can result in some serious worry about getting sleep or falling asleep. Worry of this kind can lead to spending a great amount of time in bed while giving your all to sleep forcefully. Both excess time in bed and worry can result in falling asleep and maintaining the same a challenging task. It might turn out to be a frustrating kind of night cycle that might be quite hard to break. Cognitive restructuring starts to discard this vicious cycle by simply understanding, challenging, and then changing the beliefs and thoughts that tend to contribute to sleeping problems.

Sleep Compression And Restriction

Individuals with insomnia often have the habit of spending excessive time lying on their bed awake. With the help of sleep restriction, the time that you spend in bed is restricted to reestablishing a proper and consistent schedule of sleep. The overall process is carried out with the intention to enhance the drive to fall asleep, and it can also increase the fatigue that you face during daytime temporarily. It is not at all suggested for all those people who suffer from some medical conditions as it can turn out to be bad by losing quality sleep, like seizures and bipolar disorder. The process of restricting your sleep starts by the calculation of the overall time that you spend in sleeping on any normal night with the help of a diary of sleep. The time that you spend in bed is then effectively adjusted to find out this overall amount, adding it with half an hour.

For instance, if an individual is trying to get some good sleep for eight hours a night but ends up getting only five hours, he/she will start the process by managing their bedtime to spend five hours and thirty minutes sleeping. After an individual spends most of the time sleeping in bed, they can start to increase their bedtime gradually. Sleep compression varies from the sleep restriction. It is a much simple approach. It is often suggested for elderly people. In place of just decreasing the time that you spend in bed immediately to the sleep amount that you get on any typical night, your bed time is reduced gradually. It is done until the time is close to the time they actually spend sleeping.

Stimulus Control

There are people suffering from insomnia who start to fear their bedroom, linking it with frustration along with wakefulness. Associating their bedroom along with all those habits that tend to make the overall task of sleeping more difficult for them, such as watching TV, eating, or fixing their eyes on a computer or mobile phone is a common thing in this case. The technique of stimulus control tries to bring about a change in all these associations, with the aim to reclaim the bedroom as a quiet place where you can get restful sleep. The bed is to be used only for sex and sleep during the course of the treatment. When it turns out to be very difficult to fall asleep or when patients just try to lie on their bed, wide awake for about ten minutes, they are strictly suggested to get out of their beds. You can only get back to your bed when you feel tired again. Patients are also instructed to set the alarm at the exact same time every day. Opting for daytime naps is also discouraged.

Sleep Hygiene

In this mode of treatment, you will have to bring about some changes in your basic lifestyle habits that tend to influence your quality of sleep, such as excessive drinking of alcohol, smoking, too much caffeine before bedtime, or not opting for daily exercise. You will also be provided with various tips that will help you to get better sleep. For example, ways to wind down one to two hours before going to bed.

Relaxation Technique

Relaxation techniques are quite helpful both for the mind and body. The best and the most effective techniques of relaxation are all those that be incorporated reasonably into the routine of a person. Here are some techniques of relaxation that are taught commonly in CBT-I.

- **Breathing exercise:** There are various types of breathing exercises that are taught during the process of CBT-I. All the related exercises typically involve taking deep and slow breaths. It has been found from some research that focused breathing techniques can help in enhancing breathing and slow heart rate. Also, it can help in reducing feelings of anger, depression, and anxiety.

- **PMR or progressive muscle relaxation:** It is a very widely used technique that includes tensing followed by relaxing various groups of muscle. Guided imagery or breathing exercises can also be combined easily with this technique.

- **Autogenic training:** In this process, the focus is adjusted to various body parts, and particular sensations are noticed. An individual can focus on various types of sensations like warmth, relaxation, or heaviness.

- **Biofeedback:** Biofeedback puts into use various technologies to help monitor some specific processes in your body like heart rate, brain waves, body temperature, and breathing. People can start to learn how to have more control over all these processes with the use of the information that is provided by electronic devices.

- **Meditation:** Learning to focus all your attention with the help of meditation comes with a wide range of health benefits. It helps in reducing anxiety, stress, along with increased relaxation. You can also include practices that include movements with focused attention, like tai chi and yoga.

CBT-I VS. Pills

Medications for getting sleep can turn out to be quite as effective as a short-term treatment. For instance, such medications can provide you with instant relief during a moment of high grief or stress. Some new types of sleep medications have also been approved for prolonged use. However, they might not be considered as the perfect and the best insomnia treatment for the long-term. CBT-I might be a great choice for treating insomnia in case you have sleeping problems for a long time. It can also be opted for if you feel worried or tensed about getting dependent on sleep medications, or if the medications are not much effective, or if you face some serious side effects. Unlike sleeping pills, CBT-I helps in treating insomnia by addressing the underlying cause of the same in place of just relieving the concerning symptoms. However, it takes some time, along with a bit of effort from your side, to make it work. In some of the cases, a proper combination of CBT-I and sleeping pills might turn out to be the best possible approach.

Is CBT-I Useful And Effective In Treating Insomnia?

When all the techniques are used together in combination as multicomponent CBT-I, as many as 75% - 85% of the patients with excessive insomnia can see improvements. Some of the benefits include more time spent asleep, less time needed to fall asleep, and waking up as less as possible while sleeping. The results can be maintained with passing time. According to the recommendation of the American College of Physicians, CBT-I is suggested as a first-line approach for all adult patients. In some patients, the technique has shown better results in comparison to medications. The treatment procedure of CBT-I has also shown some great and effective results in groups of people that are specifically at higher risk of experiencing excessive insomnia, for instance, pregnant women. It is also very helpful for all those people who suffer from insomnia after treatment of cancer and people with PTSD or post-traumatic stress disorder. The effectiveness of CBT in treating PTSD will be discussed in the upcoming chapters.

CBT-I has shown effectiveness with several types of insomnia. It has even shown potential benefits for all those people who suffer from short-term insomnia. It indicates that CBT-I can be quite useful in treating insomnia symptoms even when they fail to meet the criteria for the chronic stage of insomnia. While this form of treatment has shown some impressive efficacy in dealing with insomnia, it might not work the right way always. It might take some amount of time to learn properly and practice the skills that you have learned in the treatment. Some of the techniques, such as sleep restriction and stimulus control, often help in adjusting the sleeping habits quite slowly. Some individuals often find it helpful to keep track of their progress with time to see some small improvements that can easily encourage them to keep going with the treatment.

If CBT-I single-handedly cannot successfully help in bringing about some improvement in the symptoms of insomnia, the American College Of Physicians suggests having some discussion with a physician. You will have to discuss the probable benefits and risks of having sleep medications besides CBT-I treatment.

Does CBT-I Come With Any Kind Of Risk?

In order for the technique of CBT-I to be properly effective, it is essential to be always open to confront unhelpful behaviors and thoughts. Although the overall risks of the treatment are most likely to be mild, it might turn out to be quite uncomfortable at some times. Opening up and discussing painful thoughts, experiences, and feelings might be challenging. It might also cause some temporary discomfort and stress. Working in collaboration with a professional who is trained in CBT-I can help a lot to reduce the risks of this very treatment. Professionals of CBT-I are trained to provide you with tools and support so that you can easily cope up with the temporary setbacks or challenges.

How To Get CBT-I?

CBT-I is generally provided by a counselor, doctor, psychiatrist, or therapist who is properly trained in the treatment of this form. Practitioners who have experience in CBT-I can be easily found through several professional organizations like the American Board of Sleep Medicine and the Society of Behavioral Sleep Medicine. However, because of the widespread requirement of this treatment, there are not many professionals of CBT-I in order to meet the present demand. To cope up with this, researchers have come up with some new ways to offer CBT-I, for example, group, digital, and self-help structures.

Digital CBT-I

Various applications for digital CBT-I have been recently developed to adapt to the trend of treatment. It also helps a lot in reducing the overall cost of the treatment and also offers various other benefits in relation to CBT-I to a much wider audience. The Department of Veterans Affairs has its own application known as the CBT-I Coach. The application is appropriate for veterans and non-veterans alike. Online resources and smartphone-based applications offering digital CBT-I tend to vary depending on various factors. It also includes the amount of involvement and purpose that they need from a provider. Some of the resources ofer support simply while people keep working with a trained CBT-I professional in person. The other resources are completely automated and need no form of input from a professional. There are applications that come with a mixture of two, permitting people to effectively work through a program that is pre-set and have regular sessions based on telephone or e-mail feedback with a CBT-I professional.

Digital CBT-I has shown some great results in treating insomnia in adults, adolescents, and children. Improvement in the symptoms of insomnia from digital CBT-I might turn out to be similar to face-to-face discussions. But only a small number of studies have compared these two approaches directly.

Tips To Sleep With Insomnia

Properly learning about some positive sleeping habits is regarded as the core part of CBT-I. Tailoring the recommendations is done best with the help and cooperation of a CBT-I provider or professional. In the meantime, let's have a look at some of the basic tips of sleep hygiene that can be used by any person who is suffering from sleep problems.

- Try to maintain a proper sleeping schedule. Having a predictable and regular sleep schedule can always help your body to properly maintain a rhythm and also make it a lot easier to fall asleep. It includes weekends too, which are often the most common time that someone might forget about the great importance of a good night's sleep.

- Do not just lie awake in your bed. If you cannot fall asleep, try to get out of your bed and look out for something relaxing that you can do to feel tired again.

- You can also create a nightly routine. Try to give enough time to yourself to properly get ready for bed. Turn off all the electronic gadgets as early as possible and opt for some relaxing activity that can help you wind down before you go to sleep.

- Try to consider daytime activities as much as you can. All those things that you actually do during the day count. Even a small routine of exercise daily can help in getting better sleep. Also, try your best to avoid the consumption of caffeine, alcohol and eating excessively close to your bedtime.

Chapter 11: Get Relief from Stress With CBT

All of us naturally feel a specific amount of stress every day when we have to face all our daily challenges in our day to day life. When we start feeling self-confident and also to be in control, we can easily manage our way through any kind of situations that tend to trigger stress without any kind of discomfort. But in specific situations, for instance, under conditions of excessive stress or following an incident of trauma, the levels of stress can easily intensify. It is mainly because psychological and physiological stress symptoms turn out to be more severe. Some of the symptoms of stress, like heart racing, excessive worry, churning stomach, and many more, can start interfering with your structure of well-being. Also, it can make your every day or certain life situations quite difficult to deal with.

CBT or cognitive behavioral therapy can effectively help you with a brand new perspective on any kind of situation. It will allow you to get back the lost control, reduce all kinds of emotional and physiological symptoms, and adopt various effective strategies to help you deal with stressful situations of any kind with ease and confidence.

Stress In Detail

Stress is a natural part of all our lives. It can come in various forms: mental, emotional, and physical. All those stressors that are occasional are actually harmless for our health. In fact, stressors can be effectively used to push us in the direction of work for achieving important goals or even to motivate us out of a very bad situation. Moderate stress level permits the mind and body to start responding at a faster speed. But when the stressors turn out to be chronic, that is when the problem arises. It can result in mental strain along with health problems for the long term. "Stress" is often defined as a particular state of emotional, mental strain, and tension that results from certain adverse or extremely demanding circumstances.

Also, it is essential to keep a note that stress can also originate from our within. Every one of us has to always deal with various stressful situations at various points in our lives. However, the way we all get affected by all these stressors will depend on the way we learn to deal with all of them and also manage our own way through the difficult times.

Stress And Its Causes

With the fact that every individual in this world is different from the other, everyone perceives and also manifests stress in various ways. But according to some of the surveys, stress from work always tops the list. About forty percent of U.S. workers admit that they experience office

140

stress, and one-quarter admitted that work is the biggest stress source in their lives. Although, anything that results in discomfort can lead to stress in our lives. The chronic nature of stress, along with its symptoms, tends to arise when the stressor stays in its place, and the body fails to repair itself. Some of the most common life stressors that can actually have some great impact on your health are:

- Divorce

- Death of someone close

- Job loss

- Enhanced financial obligations

- Marriage

- Chronic injury or illness

- Emotional problems

- Traumatic events

As said before, stress can sometimes come from within. You can just mentally stress out yourself by thinking about the future excessively. Some patterns of thinking that can result in stress are:

- Perceptions and attitudes about your life

- Uncertainty and fear about the future

- Not being able to adapt to a change properly

- Unrealistic expectations from yourself

Symptoms Of Stress

Stress can appear in several ways that actually differ from one person to the other. Some of the common symptoms of developing stress are an increase in the rate of breathing, an increase in the level of blood pressure, slowing down of metabolism, and muscle tension. As the stress maintains its pace, additional symptoms can also be seen.

- Nausea

- Headache

- Sleep loss

- Weight gain

- Ulcers

- Cramps

- Acne

- Muscle pain

- Hair loss

- Muscle spasms

- Digestive issues

- Fainting

- Sweating

- Loss of libido

- Heart disease

- Nervous twitches

- High blood pressure

- Pain in the chest or back

Several medical conditions like fibromyalgia, type 2 diabetes, heart diseases, and also death have been linked with chronic stress.

Benefits Of CBT Therapy For Dealing With Stress

There are several benefits that come with CBT if you are willing to deal with stress.

- You can easily discover why certain situations tend to create some kind of stress response in you.

- You will easily learn how particular thinking patterns and behavior that you hold might keep you stuck and stop you from feeling a bit better in life.

- You can get the chance to find out new ways of behaving and thinking that can easily eliminate some of the stress factors completely from your life and allow you to cope up in a better way with certain unavoidable situations that might raise your levels of stress.

- You will be developing a new form of understanding along with enhanced confidence in your capability to deal with various stressful incidents or situations in your future life.

How Does CBT For Dealing With Stress Work?

CBT for relieving stress allows you to properly understand how certain patterns of behavior and thinking can enhance the levels of stress. It will also help you to readily develop some new patterns of behavior and thinking, which will permit you to identify all kinds of stress causing situations very easily. After you are done with a good CBT course for stress, you can expect to feel at ease, in proper control of yourself, and also be better at handling all your life situations.

CBT Sessions For Relieving Stress

During the first meeting, your therapist will start working with you by asking certain questions. An approach of this kind will allow you to achieve more clarity in relation to the challenges that you have been facing with stress. Also, you will be able to quickly identify a proper plan of action, which will allow you to tackle all the stressors in an effective way. During your CBT sessions, your therapist will provide you with the required help to consider some of the situations which can trigger your level of stress from an absolutely new perspective. The entire process will allow you to get knowledge about all those factors which might increase your levels of stress from a whole new angle. You will soon learn various ways of thinking, along with different types of behaviors that will permit you to reduce your levels of stress actively. It will also be increasing your capacity to deal more effectively in stressful situations without getting tensed.

Based on the history of your life, your therapist will try to interpret various events and respond to all of them in certain characteristic ways. Generally, for all those under severe stress, this kind of interpretation includes a perception of threat or danger combined with a great challenge to your ability to deal with the situations. Based on the therapist's assessment, he/she will provide you with the required help to develop some strategic plan so that you can manage your stress in a better way. Suck kind of plan would involve several approaches to alter the thoughts that produce stress and also improve your capabilities of coping with the same. For instance, a person who feels stressed about being perfect and spends most of the time watching TV, he/she can benefit from:

- Therapeutic interventions for reducing all kinds of unrealistic expectations

- Instruction for relaxation exercises

- Integration of workout regimen

Another example where a person catastrophizes his/her job setbacks and just engages in binge emotional eating can benefit from:

- Exercises in order to throw a challenge to all kinds of automatic thoughts

- Instructions of mindful eating along with diaphragmatic breathing

It can be stated that plans for management of stress tend to work the best when they are tailored in accordance to the needs of a particular person, his/her issues, along with resources.

How Many CBT Sessions Are Required?

You might wonder how much therapy you will need to address your problems of stress effectively. There are various factors that tend to influence the overall amount of CBT for stress that you might find helpful.

- The duration you have actually been dealing with stress

- Your levels of self-esteem and self-confidence

- The intensity of the situations of stress that you are dealing with

Six Sessions

It is the most commonly prescribed duration for CBT to deal with stress as it comes with the shortest time that you will need to dedicate. Despite the short span of time, you can still get some great positive outcomes with evidence. The six numbers of sessions can turn out to be most helpful when you are generally very confident. It also works when you are facing a particular kind of problem and nothing too complex. In case the kind of stress that you have been experiencing is going on for a long time, your level of self-esteem is relatively low, or there might be other factors that induce stress that you will have to deal with. In such a case, six sessions will not be able to provide you with the kind of help that you need to tackle the situations properly.

Twelve Sessions

Twelve CBT sessions are most commonly recommended when besides the situations of stress, you are also required to cope with various accompanying issues, like depression or low self-esteem. It might also turn out to be quite helpful if you are dealing with two or more than one issues that result in stress in your life.

Twenty-Four Sessions Or Even More

Twenty-four sessions or more than that is recommended when the level of stress that you are facing has been in its place for a long time. It will help in figuring out other persisting factors that tend to affect your well-being, for example, accompanying depression or anxiety.

Stress Issues That Can Be Dealt With CBT

CBT can provide you with the required help to develop the overall confidence to manage a complete range of stressful situations with great ease. It can also help you to properly improve your levels of self-confidence. Here is a list of all those situations that you can address with the help of CBT.

- Stress at career/work/ management of business

- Stress along with depression and anxiety

- Relationship stress

- Stress resulting from certain life changes

- Stress that seems to be pervasive in
  several areas of life

- Stress resulting from the desire to achieve
  success in life

- Stress resulting from relationships or
  family situations

- Stress caused by low self-confidence or
  low self-esteem

- Stress resulting from loneliness

- Stress caused by social anxiety or social
  situations

Relaxation Techniques

There are various relaxation techniques available
for you to deal with stress in a better way. Some
of the most common strategies involve
progressive muscle relaxation, diaphragmatic
breathing, relaxation, meditation, autogenic
training, visualizations, and mindfulness
practices. Generally, all our responses to these
types of exercises are kind of idiosyncratic. In
simple terms, what works for you might just not
work for some other person. As a result, it is
quite essential to opt for and try out various
techniques and just find out what works the best
for you.

Limitations Of CBT In Dealing With Stress

While CBT can provide you with some great tools to understand and deal better with the effects of stress, it might sometimes get limited in its ability to get more than this. There are cases where many people who opted for CBT failed to address the overall picture. In turn, their symptoms came back to life. It is primarily because CBT cannot treat underlying and older roots, which can be considered to be limiting the capacity to manage stress in an effective way.

Chapter 12: Overcome PTSD With CBT

PTSD or post-traumatic stress disorder is a kind of mental health condition of debilitating nature. It might tend to develop after an individual is exposed to excessive stress or any kind of traumatic event. While most people will try to resolve the distress of the short-term such as the event causes, people suffering from PTSD will keep getting affected for a longer time. PTSD can be characterized by several types of behavioral, cognitive, and physiological symptoms that are related to – avoiding reminders of any event, re-experiencing the event, and also physiological hyperarousal, like irritability or insomnia. It has been found that PTSD can affect ten percent of people at certain stages in their lives. However, rates of prevalence in individuals who have already experienced a traumatic situation or incident might be as close as hundred percent.

The symptoms of PTSD might have some significant nature of the impact on our day-to-day lives. In the majority of cases, the symptoms tend to develop right during the first month after you face a traumatic event. However, there are cases where the symptoms appeared after two to three months or even after several years. PTSD or post-traumatic stress disorder can easily develop after a frightening or distressing, or stressful event, or even after you face a long

traumatic experience. Several types of events
that might lead to PTSD are:

- Sexual or physical assault

- Serious accidents

- Abuse, along with domestic or childhood
  abuse

- Serious health problems, like being
  admitted to the ICU

- Exposure to traumatic situations or events
  at work, like remote exposure

- Conflict and war

- Experiences of childbirth, like losing a
  baby

- Torture

PTSD tends to develop in around one out of
three people who face excessive trauma. No
research has still not been able to find out why
some individuals develop the condition, whereas
others do not. But there are certain essential
factors that make some individuals more likely to
have PTSD.

Who Is At Risk?

If you have an early experience of anxiety or
depression in the past, or if you do not even get

much support from your friends and family, you are at a higher risk of developing PTSD right after you experience a traumatic event. There might also be some genetic factor that comes into play while discussing PTSD. For instance, having a parent with some mental health problem is regarded to enhance the overall chances of developing PTSD. There are various reasons that take part in the development of the condition. Let's have a look at them.

Why Does PTSD Develop?

Although it is still not clear why many individuals develop the conditions of PTSD, some possible reasons have been suggested.

Survival Mechanism

One of the first suggestions behind the development of PTSD symptoms is the result of some instinctive mechanism that is intended to provide you with the required help to survive future traumatic experiences. For instance, the flashbacks of the events that most people with PTSD tend to experience might force you to again think about any traumatic event in detail so that you can be better prepared in case it happens once more. The sheer feeling of being right on the 'edge' might develop so that you can react fast in another case of crisis. However, while all these responses might be intended towards helping you survive, they are quite unhelpful in reality. It is primarily because you won't be able to process or even move on from that traumatic experience.

High Levels Of Adrenaline

According to some latest research, it has been revealed that individuals suffering from PTSD tend to have abnormal stress hormone levels. Normally, when in a state of danger, your body produces stress hormones, such as adrenaline, to trigger certain reactions in the body. That reaction, often termed as a "fight or flight" reaction, provides help in deadening the senses and also to dull any kind of pain. People suffering from PTSD have been found to keep producing higher levels of fight or flight hormones even at times when there is no form of danger. It is thought that this might be responsible for the hyperarousal and numbed emotions that are experienced by some individuals suffering from PTSD.

Brain Changes

In all those people suffering from PTSD, some parts of the brain get involved in the processing of emotions that appear different in the brain scans. One of the primary areas of the brain that plays the part of emotions and memory is the hippocampus. In individuals with PTSD, the size of the hippocampus is found to be small in size. It is thought that the changes that take place in this area of the brain might be related to anxiety and fear, flashbacks, and memory problems. The malfunctioning of the hippocampus might prevent flashbacks along with nightmares from being processed in the right way. So, the anxiety that gets generated does not tend to even reduce over time. Proper treatment of PTSD helps in the proper processing of all the memories. So, with time, the nightmares and flashbacks disappear gradually.

CBT For PTSD

CBT or cognitive behavioral therapy is being widely used as an effective treatment option for PTSD for several years. The primary aim of CBT for PTSD is to improve the functioning of a person by altering their definite behavioral patterns, feelings, and thoughts. It is primarily structured on the very premise that advancement in any single domain can result in enhancements in the other domains. For instance, altering thoughts of detrimental nature can help in the improvement of the mood of a person and might also result in better behaviors. It is generally looked upon over a total of twelve to sixteen sessions to a group or an individual. Some of the techniques that are employed by the CBT therapists to treat PTSD are:

- Modification of cognitive distortions, such as having negative expectations or overgeneralizing bad situations. It also involves the development of more beneficial and balanced thinking ways.

- Providing the concerned patients with the reminders of the traumatic situation, under conditions that are controlled. It will allow them to tackle all of them instead of just avoiding them and their distress.

- Educating the patients regarding some of the most common reactions to trauma, teaching them to properly manage stress, planning for some potential crisis, and promoting relaxation.

All these methods are intended to provide help to a person suffering from PTSD to gain an objective understanding of the traumatic experiences and enhance their overall capability to deal with and lower behaviors of avoidance. It also helps to return their sense of self-confidence and control.

Benefits of CBT For PTSD

The useful effects of this therapy are usually assigned to modify the cognitive distortions of detrimental nature that are experienced by the patients of PTSD. A proper response to the overall therapy has also been related to physiological and functional neuroimaging, along with electroencephalographic changes, that also includes:

156

- A great decrease in the reactivity of heart rate along with an enhancement in response to blood pressure on standing in all those who suffer from PTSD after CBT.

- Non-responders to the therapy have also shown some significant poor verbal memory compared to the responders. They were found to have impaired narrative encoding.

How Can CBT Be Compared With Other Types Of Therapies?

EMDR or eye movement desensitization and reprocessing is a commonly used technique for treating PTSD that comes with somewhat similar kind of efficacy as CBT. Dr. Shapiro, who noticed successfully that certain thoughts of disturbing nature get relieved by some eye movements, developed the approach originally. The concept is primarily based on the very fact that behaviors, feelings, along with thoughts of negative nature are the result of certain memories that are processed inadequately. The technique needs the concerned person to concentrate on some images of distressing type while also getting engaged in some additional type of sensory input, generally eye movements from side-to-side. Although EMDR is generally found to be of equal efficacy as CBT, there are certain controversies that exist whether the

EMDR benefits are because of the voluntary movements of the eyes altering inhibitory/excitatory elements in the brain, or the similar CBT properties, such as exposure, along with desensitization.

CBT has already been proved to be quite useful and a safe kind of therapy for chronic and acute PTSD. It is often used after a wide range of trauma, in children, along with adults, in several cultures. It has also been often linked with somewhat better rates of remission than some other types of therapies that involve support– problem-solving therapy, hypnotherapy, structured writing therapy, supportive psychotherapy, and acupuncture. But studies showed that the percentage of patients dealing with PTSD who fail to respond well to CBT might be somewhat around fifty percent. Dropouts might be common, while several people do not even get remission. It is because of various factors, like other conditions of comorbidity, along with nature of population study.

Over the long term, the technique of CBT helps in improving the overall severity of symptoms in comparison with techniques that are not based on CBT. All those people who get CBT report have lesser intense symptoms of PTSD in comparison to all those people who get counseling of supportive nature.

Conclusion

Thank you for making it through to the end of *Cognitive Behavioral Therapy*; let's hope it was informative and was able to provide you with all of the tools you need to achieve your goals, whatever they may be.

The main aim of this guidebook is to provide you with an insight into what CBT actually is and the basics of the same. All the procedures that you will find in this book are easy to be implemented, and you can also take the help of your therapist for better results. CBT or cognitive behavioral therapy comes with special benefits for all those suffering from depression, stress, PTSD, and other psychological problems. By now, you must be well aware of the overall procedure that you will have to undertake during your therapy sessions. All that you need to do is to open up and be clear in front of your therapist.

The procedure of CBT is not complex at all, and all it needs is a little bit of cooperation from your side. In fact, the information provided in this book can act as a useful source for a friend or family member of yours who is experiencing some kind of psychological problem. Understanding and education are the key components of making any kind of treatment successful. So, make sure you attempt the treatment with a collaborative approach for better results.

Finally, if you found this book useful in any way, a review on Amazon is always appreciated!